IRAN'S GREAT AWAKENING

www.IranAliveMinistries.org

Published by Iran Alive Ministries
P.O. Box 518
Melissa, TX 75454

Interior Book Design: © Nelly Murariu at PixBeeDesign.com
Cover Design: © The Voice of the Martyrs
Front Cover Image Design © 2020 Be Design, LLC mark@bedesign.la
Photo of Woman by Rommel Canlas © Shutterstock
Photo of Hands by TRMK © Shutterstock
Photo of Cross by Suwichanon Mahahing © Shutterstock
Author Photo: © Iran Alive Ministries

Paperback ISBN-13: 978-1-7337490-4-6
ISBN-10: 1-7337490-4-7

eBook ISBN-13: 978-1-7337490-5-3
ISBN-10: 1-7337490-5-5

Library of Congress Control Number: 2019919013

Dr. Hormoz Shariat is
"The Billy Graham of Iran" – Joel C. Rosenberg

Iran's Great Awakening

HOW GOD IS USING A MUSLIM CONVERT TO SPARK REVIVAL

DR. HORMOZ SHARIAT

To my niece, Haleh
A General in the Lord's army

ENDORSEMENTS
(IN ALPHABETICAL ORDER)

Iran's political struggles and social unrest are newsworthy, but the real battle for freedom is being waged in the heavenlies. Dr. Hormoz Shariat shares his remarkable journey from Iran to the United States, and from Islam to Christianity. Out of brokenness, Hormoz found his freedom in Christ, a freedom that resulted in a powerful ministry to Persians at home and abroad. Dr. Shariat's scientific mind and understanding of both the political and the spiritual realms make him uniquely qualified to be an ambassador for Christ in the Middle East. I highly recommend this inspiring story of courage and conviction.

Dr. Neil T. Anderson

Founder and President Emeritus of
Freedom in Christ Ministries

A historical and ordained awakening of a nation coincides with God's incredible plan to use a Muslim-background believer to influence a wave of transformation in Iran. This book is a delightful, compelling, and inspiring story of commitment, perseverance and faith. A must read.

Dr. Mike Ansari

President, Heart4Iran/Mohabat TV

With a pen of fire, Hormoz Shariat describes Jesus Christ's power to change lives. In these pages, you will learn about the world's fastest-growing church, located in the world's most powerful Muslim nation. What is happening in Iran today is unprecedented in its 5,000-year history. This is Iran's Great Awakening! God is on the move.

It's time for you to learn about it, and step into the story of what He is doing!

Ray Bentley

Author, and Pastor of Maranatha Chapel

It has been my privilege to know Dr. Shariat for many years, and to serve on Iran Alive Ministries' board of directors for nearly 10 years. He is one of the few men I have known who is both an evangelist and a pastor. Hormoz has two great burdens that drive him every day: to finish his ministry well and to pass on to Iran's next generation what God has given him. You will be shocked and thrilled by what is happening in Iran. Today is the day of harvest in Iran. Will you join us in training the emerging young leaders of this massive movement of the Spirit?

We in the West have much to learn from Iran's underground church movement. Read, pray, and then act decisively.

Dr. Monroe "Monnie" Brewer

Former Missions Pastor for 36 years

East-West Ministries, Plano, Texas

Voice of the Martyrs, Bartlesville, OK

Adjunct Professor, Dallas Theological Seminary

Hormoz Shariat peels away so many misconceptions about Iran and its citizens, providing a fresh perspective on God's heart for this extraordinary nation. Iran is not a country Christians should fear, but rather, be ready to invest, if need be, their lives to see the Gospel transform all Iranians and strengthen His church. Hormoz is a dear friend and ministry partner whose life exemplifies a deep passion for making disciples of all nations and bringing glory to the Great I Am.

Floyd Brobbel

President, The Voice of the Martyrs, Canada

Few nations are of greater consequence to God's end-time plan for the earth than Iran. Within this fascinating nation, there is nothing as potent as today's awakening church. And within the Iranian church, there is no one who has made a greater impact than Dr. Hormoz Shariat. His influence is breathtaking, his story is enthralling, and his insights are crucial for us all. *Iran's Great Awakening* is a gift of pure gold for those who love the Lord and understand the remarkable times we live in.

Dr. David Cannistraci

Gateway City Church, San Jose, California

This is absolutely a must read. Dr. Hormoz has poured out his heart, but more importantly he has opened our eyes to the incredible harvest that is about to come to Iran. This harvest will change the course of the Middle East! This book will awaken your heart.

Dr. Robert W. Carman D.D.

President of Victory World Missions

We live in a world filled with chaos and devoid of spiritual courage. Into the maelstrom and swirling storms of cultural dissonance comes the powerful voice of Hormoz Shariat. Speaking with clarity and candor, Shariat stirs the heart and compels our hands. It is one thing to be inspired, quite another to be empowered. Hormoz speaks with the integrity of a man seasoned by cultural battles but with the compassion of a man infused with God's presence. This is the voice of a statesman for the Kingdom of Heaven, a man of deep conviction in a season of desperate need.

Rev. Paul Louis Cole, D.Th.
ChristianMensNetwork.com

Inside these pages, you will discover a true story of a radical conversion, of the effect of amazing grace on a human heart. From an unlikely background, Dr. Hormoz Shariat has become a modern-day Apostle Paul. This is a brilliant tale of the author's personal journey to Jesus Christ in a Muslim-dominated world. You will witness Hormoz's unstoppable passion to reach the seemingly unreachable, and you will be encouraged in your own walk with Christ to do the same. Get your copy of *Iran's Great Awakening* and spark a revival in your community today!

Billy Crone
Author, Pastor, and Media Leader

When you think of Iran, *terrorism* probably comes to your mind first. But did you know that Iran has the fastest-growing church in the world right now? Hormoz Shariat is right in the middle of this historic movement of God! God took a Muslim from Tehran and brought him to faith in Christ. Hormoz's life was changed radically, but God was just getting started.

Today, Hormoz Shariat is president of Iran Alive, and the Spirit of God is all over this man. He is a winsome, warm, and humble powerhouse for Christ who is bringing the Gospel to thousands of Iranians every day through television. I've been to Iran, and the people are truly loving, gracious, and welcoming. I believe Iranians are more open to Jesus than any other people on the planet. Hormoz and his wonderful wife, Donnell, have been selected and raised up for this special moment in time. He truly is the Billy Graham of Iran. I love Hormoz and have been privileged to be his ministry partner for more than a decade.

Iran's Great Awakening is a thrilling book! I highly recommend it to you. And be sure and grab a copy for your pastor. Read it and you'll understand the real story in Iran. You'll also see how God can take one man and use him to be His voice to a nation on the brink of disaster. Iran needs Jesus! Hormoz Shariat has dedicated his life to making that happen.

Thank you, Hormoz, for giving us a bird's-eye view of the miracle that is Jesus's church in Iran. Nobody knows this miracle better than you!

Tom Doyle

Author of *Dreams and Visions*, *Killing Christians*, and *Standing in the Fire*
President of Uncharted Ministries

Seldom does a nation experience a radical spiritual transformation like the one we have seen in Iran over the past fifty years. And no one has been more instrumental in that awakening and transformation than Dr. Shariat, whose ministry has impacted hundreds of thousands of Iranian lives. His story and insight are invaluable to understanding what God is doing in these last days to radically change the Muslim world.

Mani Erfan

President & Founder
Mani Erfan Ministries

Dr. Hormoz Shariat is not only one of the most humble, caring, and generous people I have ever known, he is on a very short list of those whom the Lord is using to transform an entire population with the hope of Christ. It is not an overstatement to call Hormoz "The Pastor of a Nation," because Iran's people have been deeply impacted by the Lord's work through Iran Alive Ministries, in every corner of the country and throughout the Persian world.

Ken Fifer, D.Min.

Missions Pastor, Bent Tree Bible Fellowship

It is impossible to consider the miracle of salvation pouring out among Iranian people without mentioning the visionary and pioneering work of Brother Hormoz Shariat. I commend this book to all who have a heart for what God is doing in Iran and among the Iranian diaspora!

David Garrison

Missionary and Author of *A Wind in the House of Islam*

Wow, what a fantastic book! It is engaging with every turn of the page. The author shares his early years as a Muslim, his involvement in the protests that helped overthrow the Shah of Iran, the execution of his brother in an Iranian prison, and his becoming a Christian. And he warns about what is coming in the near future for Iran. Every chapter is challenging, yet encouraging. Read this book. You will be glad that you did.

Tom Hughes

Lead Pastor, 412 Church

Founder, Hope For Our Times

Through Hormoz's life story, you'll come to experience the fascinating grace of God's faithfulness and how God, in His mercy, directs a man's steps. God calls us and chooses to manifest His life through us by the Holy Spirit's power when we yield to Him. In dying to ourselves we find true, eternal life in Jesus and His resurrection power. May millions in Iran be saved through the power of the Cross and the cleansing blood of our Lord and Savior, Jesus Christ!

Kevin Jessip

President, Global Strategic Alliance

Iran's Great Awakening will give you hope and confidence about the country's future. This is not a book that artificially makes you feel good. It is a book about the powerful demonstration of a move of God that is transforming the lives of thousands of Iranians every day. As God leads the movement through Dr. Shariat, Iran is now the fastest- growing Christian nation in the world.

Shariat's journey from Islam in Iran to Jesus is moving. He came to America to earn his doctorate in technology at USC. Upon graduation, he moved to Silicon Valley and a high-paying technology job. Little did he know how God would ultimately use him.

I have watched God's call on his life for more than twenty-five years. God called Dr. Shariat to disciple His people and plant the largest Iranian churches in America. Now, through a TV satellite ministry to Iran, God has moved mightily to empower the fastest-growing Jesus movement in the world. Reading *Iran's Great Awakening* will inspire and give you hope!

Bryce Jessup

President Emeritus,

William *Jessup* University

For many years I have been a friend and admirer of Hormoz Shariat, and a partner to his work in Iran. I will tell you plainly that no one else in the world can match his heart, passion, and knowledge when it comes to reaching the lost of Iran. What Hormoz shares in this book will absolutely astound you and reveal the unfolding of God's secret plan for Iran in the last days.

Jeff King

President, International Christian Concern

Persecution.org

This is a powerful testament to God's calling on our lives and His faithfulness in leading us to fulfill the promises that He has placed in our lives for His glory. Challenging and thoughtful applications in each chapter make this a great study tool for personal development or for group application.

Pastor Tong Liu

Founder and Senior Pastor of River of Life Christian Church

The Gospel is victorious inside Iran despite the Islamist regime's intense opposition to God's Word and His people. No amount of imprisonment, torture, or killing has slowed the Gospel's advance. *Iran's Great Awakening* is a critical part of the story of history's greatest move of God among Muslims. It should be read by everyone so that all may know that John 1:5 is true in Iran: The light of Christ shines in Islam's deepest darkness, and the darkness has not overcome it.

Cole Richards

President, The Voice of the Martyrs (vom.org)

Behind the iron curtain of the Islamic Republic of Iran, a movement is spreading—one that has the ayatollahs terrified. Though they work to extinguish it, it continues to spread like wildfire. I'm speaking of Iran's underground church, the fastest-growing revival in the world. For decades, Pastor Hormoz Shariat has been one this movement's shining lights. Hearing his story, and the story of the Iranian Christians, will ignite the flames of revival in your heart. The Western church needs to read this book.

Joel Richardson

New York Times best-selling author,
filmmaker, and speaker

Dr. Shariat has written an honest and powerful testimony of his life's journey. This book is more than the author's personal testimony; it explores deep truths that are vital to the body of Christ today. Each chapter carries biblical principles of the cost and rewards of true discipleship. These truths penetrate the very heart and nature of what it means to be a Christian today. This book is a must read for Christians today.

Drs. Frederic and Susan Rowe

Founders, The Global Watch

Dr. Hormoz Shariat is a humble servant with a heart of gold. The Lord has given him a mighty voice to spread the Gospel of Jesus Christ. Great things, such as miracles, healings, and visions have been accomplished through his steadfast efforts to evangelize the lost throughout the world, especially Iran. Countless lives have been inspired, and souls have been saved through his television shows and related teachings. Iran has truly come alive because of his ministerial efforts through Iran Alive Ministries! *Iran's Great Awakening* is a must read, guaranteed to motivate many readers to greatness.

Bill Salus

Founder of Prophecy Depot Ministries

This book is the most informative and inspirational book I have ever read on what God is doing in Iran. Pastor Hormoz Shariat masterfully shares startling testimonies and spiritual insights that he gained from the Scriptures and his work on the ground in Iran. Equally riveting is Hormoz's pilgrimage from influential Silicon Valley scientist to church planter to international apostolic worker. Once you pick up this book, you won't be able to put it down. Get ready to be inspired and empowered.

Dr. Ed Silvoso

Founder and CEO of Transform Our World/Harvest Evangelism and author of *Ekklesia* and *Anointed for Business*

Wow! What an incredible and powerful testimony of God's amazing and abounding grace! This book is a living testament of what God did through one man's radical obedience to His calling. Dr. Hormoz's life story is truly a message for our generation. And, like the early apostles, he reminds us that no matter how difficult it seems at times to complete God's callings and assignments, He is always faithful. I've had the privilege of knowing and being friends with Dr. Hormoz for two decades, and have had the pleasure of serving alongside him. I have been deeply moved by the depth and substance of his life, reflected so honestly in this book.

Truly, his life exemplifies simple obedience to God (which is the highest form of worship), persistence, personal consecration, courage, and personal sacrifice. For the humble Dr. Hormoz, of course, it's an honor, not a sacrifice, to serve the Lord and love His people. His story reminds me of a quote by the great missionary David Livingstone: "Why is it when an earthly king commissions us, we consider it an honor, but when the Heavenly King commissions us, we call it a sacrifice?"

Yes, in many ways, Dr. Hormoz, his family, and those who have stood with him, have made sacrifices along the way, yet they recognize the privilege of God's calling them. This is a must-read book! May you be deeply moved and provoked in your own life and journey in the Lord as you read and digest this real-life testament to God's love, grace, and mercy.

Doug Stringer

Founder, Somebody Cares America

Jesus promised, "I will build my church, and the gates of Hades will not overcome it." From an early 21st-century American perspective, one could be tempted to doubt these words. But for those who lift up their eyes to see what God is doing across the earth, all doubt fades. He is moving with power to fulfill this promise. Perhaps the hottest spot on the map of the Spirit's moving is Iran. Dr. Shariat is not only uniquely positioned to describe the work of the Spirit there, he is one of its chief catalysts.

I pray every reader will be inspired to live more boldly for the King and His kingdom as a result of this book.

Clyde Taber

Executive Director, Visual Story Network

I have thanked God often for pastor Hormoz Shariat, for his heart for God, his passion for Iran, his zeal for the Gospel, and his unique gift in evangelism. Hormoz has been at the forefront of a great movement of God in Iran. If you would like a front row seat for this spiritual revolution in the Persian-speaking world, read this book!

Rev. Sasan Tavassoli, Ph.D.

Pars Theological Center

What's happening in Iran today is unprecedented. It is just like the Lord to move so powerfully through a people governed by such an ill-inspired regime. Most incredibly, the testimony of the blood-won Iranian church is already impacting the nations and pressing us into a beautiful expression of God's eternal purposes in our day and time. Dr. Shariat's testimony will encourage you. His clarity will edify you. This book will empower you. Something incredible is taking place; let it not be said of us that we did not use every opportunity to be part of it.

Dalton Thomas

Founder/President, FAI

You will be inspired by the story of Dr. Hormoz Shariat! You will weep as he shares his struggles and shout for joy when you see God's victory in his life. What an amazing story of an ardent researcher who was a Muslim and came to faith in Christ! His walk with Christ and his ministry will challenge you to dig deep and find the true source of success. Your life will be enriched and your vision expanded as you read what God has done in Dr. Shariat's life.

Dr. Sammy Tippit

Author and International Evangelist

Dr. Hormoz Shariat heard the words of God: *"Iran is ready."* Be prepared to experience a startling testimony, a big vision, and the enormous personal obstacles that did not stop this brother in Christ from bringing the Gospel to a spiritually starving Iran. I highly recommend you take the journey to discover how a million Iranians will embrace Jesus as Messiah through Dr. Shariat's steadfast faith and media outreach.

Walt Wilson

Founder and Chairman

Global Media Outreach

Iran's House Church Movement has created the fastest-growing church in the world. In the forty years since the Islamic Revolution, the number of Iranian followers of Christ (from Muslim backgrounds) has jumped from fewer than 500 to over one million! This is a mighty move of the Holy Spirit, in cooperation with dedicated men and women of God. Dr. Hormoz Shariat is one of them. He could have been a millionaire, but he left his lucrative career and dedicated himself to serving the Lord Jesus Christ. Through his 24-hour TV ministry, he has shared the saving message of the Gospel with millions of Iranians.

I wish Brother Hormoz many more victories in presenting the Savior of the world and the King of Kings to many more millions of Farsi-speaking people.

Brother Luke Yeghnazar

Eternal Life Agape Ministries, Inc.

Table of Contents

FOREWORD

I CONSIDER **HORMOZ SHARIAT** to be the Billy Graham of Iran.

He is far and away the most watched and most influential Iranian evangelist in the world, and his story is well worth reading.

In his day, Billy Graham preached the Gospel of Jesus Christ clearly and unequivocally in stadiums all over the world. Sometimes 40,000 or 50,000 or even 100,000 people or more would come each night to hear Dr. Graham speak the truths of God's Word. Yet the most widely listened-to and fruitful evangelist in the history of the world was never able to travel into Iran to preach the message of eternal salvation, because to do so was (and is) utterly illegal.

But now God has opened an extraordinary door. Twenty-four hours a day, seven days a week, and 365 days a year, Hormoz Shariat and his Iran Alive Ministries colleagues broadcast satellite television programs in Farsi (the language of the Iranian people), sharing the Gospel, teaching in-depth Bible studies, and taking live phone calls from Muslims, who call at great personal risk. These Muslims are so desperate to know if Jesus is God, and so hungry to have their souls and bodies healed by Him, that they are willing to make the call even though they know they could be discovered by the secret police, arrested, tortured, and even killed for showing interest in Christianity.

Because Hormoz and his team are broadcasting programs unlike anything on Iranian state-run television, millions of Iranians are watching every day. They watch in the privacy of their homes, hungry for the truth and grateful for men and women willing to speak the truth in love.

Hormoz's satellite network also broadcasts Christian worship services into Iran, right over the heads of the ayatollahs and the mullahs and the Iranian intelligence services. Many secret believers in Iran are too scared to go to a church, fearing that the secret police might catch them. Many Muslim converts are too scared to play Christian music in their homes or sing too loudly, fearing that their neighbors might hear them. For some of them, the church services that Hormoz's network broadcasts are the only times of worship and fellowship they have. And for Muslims who are curious about Christianity, such services give them a safe window into a spiritual world of hope to which they feel increasingly drawn.

I had the joy of meeting Hormoz nearly fifteen years ago. He had become interested in my novels and in my first non-fiction book, *Epicenter*, in which I explained a number of Bible prophecies and shared my conviction that the Lord will, one day, draw millions upon millions of Jews and Muslims into the Kingdom of Christ by the power of His Holy Spirit. For some reason, Hormoz graciously invited me to visit him in a secure, undisclosed location. I gratefully accepted his offer, and am so glad I did.

For me, a Jewish follower of Jesus, it was incredibly moving to meet such a remarkable Iranian follower of Christ and his family and his staff. It was amazing to see how God was using them to reach the nation of Iran, the people they love so dearly, with the life-changing message of the Gospel.

Most remarkable to me was to learn that Hormoz did not grow up in a Christian home, hoping to be an evangelist. To the contrary, he was an Iranian-born Shia Muslim. His wife was an American-born convert to Islam who had come to Iran for work. The two met in Tehran. That's where they were married. In 1979, they were members of the Iranian Revolution, marching with millions of other Iranians in Tehran's streets, shouting, "Death to America! Death to the Shah!" And then, as you'll read, they thought, *Well, maybe not Death to America quite yet. We'd like to go to graduate school over there.*

What follows is an extraordinary and truly miraculous journey. This is the story of how God led Hormoz and Donnell Shariat from Iran to America, from Shia Islam to faith in the Lord Jesus Christ, from students of the Quran to teachers of the Bible, from people with no background in media production to pioneers in Gospel satellite television. What's more, this is the story of two lost and broken people (a couple whose marriage was in the process of blowing up), whom God not only saved and healed but called to become leaders of a worldwide movement of Muslims turning to Christ.

I am humbled to call Hormoz and Donnell my friends. They have welcomed me into their home. They have introduced me to their family and friends and staff and board members. We have prayed together. We have studied the Scriptures together. We have spoken at conferences together. I've appeared on their network several times, teaching the Bible and answering questions on live broadcasts. My wife, Lynn, and I have even had the honor of hosting Hormoz in Jerusalem, Israel, on his first foray into the Holy Land, where he shared his story at an Epicenter Conference organized by The Joshua Fund, a ministry we established several years ago.

For years, I have been urging Hormoz to write a book that would share his story in detail, and to explain the vision that the Lord has given him for the salvation of the Muslim world—particularly the transformation of Iran from the world's most dangerous terrorist state to a nation in love with Jesus. Finally, Hormoz has come to his senses and done what I've been asking for so long!

The book you hold in your hands is not only worth reading; it's worth sharing with others. Don't simply read it. Write about it. Talk about it. Discuss it on social media. Absorb its message and pass it on to others.

More people need to understand how much God loves the world's 1.6 billion Muslims. More people need to learn about the work of Iran Alive Ministries and the power of Gospel satellite television. And far more people need to be involved in praying for (and financially investing in) the effort to reach every Iranian and all Muslims with the Gospel of Jesus Christ.

I sincerely hope that this book, *Iran's Great Awakening*, will be used by God to educate and mobilize a far larger movement of Christians to love the Muslim people, and to more deeply appreciate God's great power to seek and save the lost.

I must confess that Hormoz is driving me to jealousy me because (so far) so many more Muslims than Jews are coming to faith in Christ. Indeed, more Muslims have come to Christ in the past fifty years than during the previous fourteen centuries. As a Jewish follower of Jesus, and citizen of the State of Israel, I certainly believe the words of the Apostle Paul in Romans 11:26. I have no doubt that one day, "All Israel will be saved." Right now, I see a great awakening underway in Iran, and not yet in Israel. But that's another reason I love Hormoz and the book he has written. Because God has taught him lessons that my colleagues and I need to learn as we work to reach our people and seek God for an Israeli awakening.

There is one other reason I believe this book is important: its emphasis on biblical prophecy. Sadly, most Christians don't study prophecy. Yet 27 percent of the Bible, more than one in four verses, is prophetic. Most Christians ignore these Scriptures because they feel they are too complicated or controversial. That's a profound mistake. Every verse of Scripture is inspired by God and useful to us. There are important things about the future of specific nations that God urgently wants us to know. That's why He gave us these prophecies. And woe to us if we ignore them and thus are unprepared when dramatic events eventually come to pass. We will all give an account to the Lord one day. Knowing this, do we really want to have paid scant attention to one-quarter of what God is telling us in His Word? To have failed to live in light of the critical truths contained in these passages?

In this book, Hormoz explains the biblical prophecies about Iran. He explores the passage in Jeremiah 49 that explains how God will judge the leaders of Elam (Iran) and then move His throne there. He also addresses the prophecies found in Ezekiel, chapters 38 and 39, in which God (in the "last days") vows to judge an alliance of nations seeking to attack Israel, an alliance partly led by a nation known as Persia.

What exactly do these passages say? What do they mean? And how should they motivate us to live differently for Christ? Some authors and Bible teachers might shy away from such matters. Not my friend Hormoz. To the contrary, he deals with them head-on, with courage and candor. For this I love him all the more.

May the Lord bless you for picking up this book and reading it thoroughly and digesting it carefully. May the Lord bless you even more for letting the Holy Spirit ignite a passion inside you to reach every Iranian, indeed every Muslim, with the message of Jesus.

Today, the mere mention of Iran too often conjures up thoughts of war, rumors of war, terror, and tragedy. But Hormoz and I believe that a new day is coming. Soon, possibly very soon, the Lord Jesus will move His throne into the heart of Iran. He will transform that country for His glory. He will send many Persian people into the world as His servants and His witnesses. The Islamic Republic will become the Christian Republic. The Islamic Revolution will become a Gospel Revolution.

In the pages ahead, Hormoz testifies first-hand that this prophetic, supernatural transformation has already begun in Iran. But it is far from complete. More is coming. Much more. He wants you to be of it, and so do I. So read on, dear friend, and discover Iran's Great Awakening for yourself.

Joel C. Rosenberg

Jerusalem, Israel
January 10, 2020

PART I

MY JOURNEY OUT OF ISLAM

CHAPTER 1

"DEATH TO THE SHAH, DEATH TO AMERICA"

I WAS BORN into a Muslim family in Tehran, Iran in 1955. My grandfather had been an Islamic religious leader. He passed away when my dad was just a kid.

Today, in the city of Semnan, there is a mosque that was built and dedicated to Islam by my grandfather's grandfather in 1826. Called Sultan's Mosque, it stands as the oldest and most prominent mosque in the region.

My grandfather (who lived from 1865 to 1920) served as the mosque's custodian for much of his life, and he also directed the upkeep of other buildings and lands in the area.

After my grandfather died, his nephew assumed those responsibilities. In fact, that mosque, along with assorted other schools, buildings, and lands, were under the care of someone from my family until the 1970s. (After the Islamic revolution of 1978-1979, the mosque was taken over by the new government and renamed Imam's Mosque, but was also referred to as Khomeini's Mosque.)

My parents were educators. My dad was a high school principal, and my Mom was a teacher. They were Muslims, but they never forced their faith on me. I remember my Mom always telling me, "Don't be a bigot or closed-minded. Never accept or reject anything before you study and understand it."

I held on to Islamic beliefs and practiced them until I was twelve. At that time, I started thinking, "What effect do these practices, such as fasting and ritual prayers, have on me?" I did not (and still don't) like repeating things mindlessly if they do not add to my life. I had been following these rituals, but they were doing nothing for me. They did not change me or affect my relationships.

I wondered, *Where is God*? These rituals were certainly not connecting me to Him.

So I decided to discard the Islamic rituals, in favor of simply trying to be a good person and focusing on my studies.

I decided I wanted to be a scientist. I dreamed of going to the United States of America to pursue graduate studies. I hoped to earn a Ph.D. in science and then become a research scientist at one of the top research centers.

I worked hard and became the top student in my class at Kharazmi High School. Then I was admitted to the region's top technical school, Aryamehr University, which is now named Sharif University of Technology. (Incidentally, "Aryamehr" means "lover of the Aryan race," and it was one of the Shah's nicknames. The school was renamed after the revolution. Sharif Vaghefi was one of the martyrs killed during the revolution.)

"DEATH TO SHAH, DEATH TO AMERICA!"

While in college, I met Donnell, this brave American girl from Oregon who had moved to Tehran and was working at DuPont, the well-known global science company. Donnell was a nominal

Christian, and when we decided to get married, she converted to Islam.

She was touched by the devotion of Muslims. She admired their focus on their faith and their families. When she compared Islam to the lukewarm Christianity she saw in her church, she was drawn to Islam. Of course, she needed to convert to marry me, but her devotion to the faith was real. We were married in Tehran on October 23, 1977.

In 1978, I finished my last semester at technical school—and not a moment too soon. That summer, turmoil erupted on the streets of Tehran, and the demonstrations forced my school to shut down.

I should note that I was not a leader but an active participant in the protests. I supported the effort, because that's what all my peers were doing.

For the four years I was on campus, I shared this mind-set with my fellow students: "We need do something for the good of our country because the Shah of Iran is corrupt."

It wasn't about politics; it was about our genuine love for our nation. Plus, it was our job as students to oppose *something*!

On September 8, 1978, (a day that became known as Black Friday), the Shah's army opened fire on a group of protesters, killing and wounding hundreds.

My new wife faced death during this season of protest. Twice.

During a street demonstration outside her job at DuPont, Donnell heard bullets crash through her window and ricochet off a wall. Some of those bullets barely missed her head. Later, slugs were found in the trash bin near her desk.

Weeks later, her life was spared again. A few minutes after she finished dining in a restaurant in Tehran's Argentina Square, a bomb exploded, killing many diners.

The protests and violence continued through the fall of 1978.

I faced a dilemma. I wanted to be on the streets, supporting the demonstrations. But I knew that I could be shot and killed as a result. Eventually, my sense of duty to my country overcame my fears. Donnell and I decided to join the demonstrators, despite the danger.

It's important to note that the revolution began with students and other young people. Eventually, the oil workers joined effort, going on strike, as did some government employees.

When it looked like we might actually topple the powerful Shah and bring in a democratic government, more older men joined.

However, most of the protesters were brave young men and women who protested peacefully.

By December 1978, the Shah decided to stop responding violently to the demonstrators. This caused our resistance to grow in numbers, and in boldness. Various factions of the resistance began to unite and organize.

In the beginning, this revolutionary movement was not Islamic at all. There were many opposition groups, including the intellectuals (mostly university students and graduates), the mujahideen (a militant Islamic group), the Fadaian (a militant/terrorist Marxist group that had been trying to topple the government for 25 years), the Tudeh Party (a communist group), and several other Islamic groups, some liberal and conservative.

These disparate groups had differing philosophies and beliefs, but they all knew that they would need to find some common ground and purpose if they wanted to bring down the Shah, who was backed by the United States. The biggest question was *how* to bring him *down*.

Eventually, the resistance found common ground in the Islamic faith. Even the intellectuals like me (who didn't practice the faith in our daily lives) held positive feelings about Islam. We believed that Islam was a good religion, even if it wasn't our personal religion.

Thus, Islam became the revolution's focal point. Soon, a rather obscure Islamic leader named Ruhollah Khomeini became the face of the revolution. (Americans came to know this man as Ayatollah Khomeini.)

Khomeini had been exiled by the Shah in 1964, and he was living in Paris, France, when the revolution erupted. He accepted the role as "leader of the opposition."

He met with the leaders of all the opposition groups—even the atheists—assuring them that he had no desire to lead Iran after the revolution succeeded. When the Shah was gone, Khomeini promised to step aside and let Iran be governed democratically. This promise pleased everyone in the resistance, so Khomeini received a promise of full support.

This sudden unity shocked the Shah's regime. It also shocked President Jimmy Carter and his administration. American leadership didn't realize just how unpopular the Shah was. And no one expected the Shah to face such a large and unified movement.

When President Carter and his team saw millions of people protesting, the United States withdrew its support of the Shah. They encouraged (or perhaps forced) the Shah to step down and leave the country—before Iran suffered any more bloodshed.

The Shah had become so unpopular that even the students and other intellectuals became militant. Donnell was so shaken by the two violent attacks she experienced that she donned the chador (an Islamic cloak) and joined me on Tehran's streets, shouting, "Death to Shah. Death to America!" with the rest of the mobs.

However, while my lips were proclaiming death to the United States, in my heart I was pleading, "But not yet. I want to get my Ph.D. from a good American university!"

Indeed, this was a time of profound internal conflict for me. It was my dream to attend school in America, but I knew I would hate myself if I sat at home and failed to join the other university students in their heartfelt protests. I didn't want to be disloyal to my country. But I also didn't want to get killed while protesting. I should add here that today my wife and I joyfully sing "God Bless America." Those days of anti-America sentiments are long gone.

The Shah left Iran in January of 1979, and we all felt that our troubles were behind us. The opposition unified under Khomeini, and we expected Iran to become a democratic country in short order.

I hoped to resume my plans of earning a doctoral degree from an American university and becoming a research scientist.

I had applied to and was admitted to the University of Southern California (USC). In late January of 1979, Donnell and I left the chaos of Iran to build a better life for ourselves, to pursue the American dream.

WHAT WERE YOUR CHILDHOOD DREAMS?

I am not and have never been a fan of empty rituals, which bring no personal benefit. If you practice something over and over and it doesn't change you, maybe you are searching for truth and meaning in the wrong place.

I had a dream from childhood that God would use me to do something great through science to impact people's lives. It was a God-given vision and He directed me to fulfill that vision in a better way--through the sharing of His Gospel.

What about you? What were you passionate about when you were younger? Have you given up on those dreams? Have they withered and died within you?

Often our passions, our dreams, are from God. They reflect how God has designed you and me and what He wants from our lives.

Now, you might say, "I don't think much about my childhood dreams because I wasn't a believer back then. However, while you might not have known God, He knew you. He called you even before you were born. (See Jeremiah 1:5 and Ephesians 2:10.)

Take time to review those childhood dreams with God right now.

Pray, "Dear Lord, I had dreams in my youth that are now forgotten and buried under the burdens of this life. Were they truly from You? Did You design me for them? If so, please resurrect them in my heart and enable me to pursue them with Your strength and direction, and for Your glory."

When Donnell and I came to America, we were starving for change. We dreamed of making a better life for ourselves. We pursued that goal the best way we knew how—through education and being open-minded.

What about you? Are you hungry for change? Are you open to new spiritual truths? No matter how hard your life may have been as a child or how many miles you have traveled to get where you are now, I want you to know that you are not alone. We all have unique paths to walk, but there are universal truths we can rely on throughout our journeys.

I know that my life is a bit radical. Most people reading this book have never shouted "Death to Shah, Death to America" on the streets of Tehran.

But I know that many of us feel embarrassed by certain parts of our life stories. Please don't hide any part of your story, for it makes you who you are today.

I believe your life is unique and your story is worth sharing including the good, bad, and the embarrassing.

I share my story (the good, the bad, and the embarrassing), because I value truth. I left my family in Iran to begin a new search for truth and a better life for Donnell and me.

I believe your life is unique and your story is worth sharing: the good, bad, and the embarrassing.

At the end of this book, I will share questions for you to reflect on, questions connected to each chapter.

As a research scientist by trade (and by passion), I believe God has so much more for you and for me if we are willing and open-minded enough to reflect, study, and research.

Psalm 32:8 assures us, "I will instruct you and teach you in the way which you should go; I will counsel you with My eye upon you." This verse has always held deep meaning for me, because it gives me the warmest feeling that God is my father.

My earthly father was not involved in my life at all. He was very distant. As a middle child in a large family, I was mostly ignored. I was encouraged to be "the quiet child," to study hard and avoid causing any trouble.

As a result, I felt like I grew up without a father. I always wanted a male presence in my life, a father figure who would teach me how to live and give me wisdom to make the right decisions and have the right attitude.

That never happened, but it didn't stop me from pursuing my dreams, living my life, and learning from good books—as well as from my mistakes.

Eventually, I found the best book in the world (the Bible) and the best father (God). God has never left me. He has always guided me, even in the worst crises and most heart-wrenching decisions of my life.

CHAPTER 2

"YOU ARE AN INFIDEL AND YOU WILL GO TO HELL!"

THE DRIVE DOWN the San Gabriel Mountains provides a beautiful view of Los Angeles. It was January 1979, and I was full of excitement and great optimism for my future. Iran was on its way to becoming a democracy, and I was well on my way to achieving my dreams. But something was missing in my life.

Life in the United States was comfortable, but I was not satisfied. Like many others who came to America, I expected to live happily ever after. I didn't expect to feel so miserable inside.

I was achieving my dreams, so why wasn't I happy? Why did I feel empty inside? Why did life feel meaningless? I thought that if I got a degree and found a good job, I would be happy.

To me, there were only two kinds of people: those who achieved their life goals and those who did not. If I were falling short of my goals, then I would have reason to feel frustrated. But I was achieving my dreams, yet still feel empty and depressed.

I began to question the meaning of life. I thought, *You get a degree and find a good job. Then you buy a house and a nice car. After that, you get a bigger house and a nicer car. And then you die! Is that all there is to life? If so, life is so empty and vain.*

I needed a bigger purpose than a degree, a good job, and a comfortable life.

Meanwhile, Donnell and I were facing major problems in our marriage. We were considering divorce and had even set a date for separating.

I blamed all my negative thoughts on a bad marriage. Maybe if I got a divorce, my life would get better.

But when I was truly honest with myself, I sensed that my problem was deeper and wider than my marriage. My problem was with life itself. Mine had no meaning. I needed a bigger purpose than a degree, a good job, and a comfortable life.

I realized that I had been ignoring my Islamic faith. I had forgotten God. I reasoned, *I should go back to my Islamic faith. It must be true. After all, look at how Islam defeated the Shah and the powerful United States. This could not have happened in such a powerful way and in such a short time without God's help.*

But wait a minute, I reminded myself, *there was a time when I truly and sincerely practiced Islam, and it did nothing for me personally.*

I was so confused. On the outside, Islam appeared powerful and true. On the inside, it seemed to hold no practical power. Therefore, it could not be true. My anxiety boiled down to one question: Was Islam true or not?

I concluded that Islam must be true, and that I had been wrong to doubt it. Those doubts had begun when I was about 12, and I reasoned that 12 was too young for someone to decide that Islam was irrelevant to daily life. I must have missed something about Islam's doctrines and practices.

I decided to study the Quran one more time—but as a researcher this time. I would be objective and study with an open and bias-free mind. I knew my intelligence and sincere heart would not lead me astray.

If there was truth in the Quran, I should be able to find it.

I purchased a Quran (in Farsi and Arabic) and started studying it with a new zeal and hunger for the truth. I decided that if I found God in the Quran, then I would dedicate the rest of my life to serving Allah and telling others about Islam.

It took me only three months to complete an intense study of the Quran. I already knew most of the material I encountered, but I did learn a few new things.

But my heart was still empty. I was not changed. What's more, I still hadn't encountered the God I searched for so diligently.

After reading the Quran, I concluded that either there is no God or that God has nothing to do with our daily personal lives.

At the time, I believed that Islam was the world's preeminent religion. Thus, if I didn't find God in the Quran, I might as well ignore the rest of the world's "inferior" religions.

But then something in my heart told me to study the Bible, even though I thought it would be a waste of time.

Eventually, because of my intellectual pride, I decided to read the Bible so that I could tell others I had read it. When I began reading the Bible, I expected to finish it in three to four days, because I was willing to invest 12- to 16-hour days to complete my task. However long it took, I didn't expect to discover anything I didn't already know. I read Genesis rather quickly and then jumped to the first book of the New Testament, Matthew.

I encountered the real Jesus in the Bible.

I encountered the real Jesus in the Bible. I expected to find the *prophet* Jesus, someone who said things that were already in the Quran or things inferior to the Quran.

I was wrong. Jesus seemed to be *more* than a prophet. He seemed too proud to be a prophet. After all, He pointed people to Himself rather than to God. Prophets were supposed to be humble people who give a message and then call others to follow and glorify God.

Jesus made too many "I" statements. I discounted His miracles, because, as a scientist, I believed they were made up, perhaps written after His death to increase His stature as a prophet.

I also struggled with His teachings. I struggled to understand them. Jesus's words were fresh, beautiful, and powerful—especially the Sermon on the Mount, which touched me deeply. I loved it. And I hated it.

I liked the beauty of the sermon, but I hated its lack of applicability to my life.

I protested, "This is not practical. Who can live like this? This is beautiful poetry, but I'm not looking for poetry. I'm looking for something that works; this does not work!"

I told Jesus, "These standards of Yours are impossible. Nobody can live up to them. They are beautiful, but who can do it? Who can control his mind at all times? I'm looking for real-life advice that works. This is not it."

I had planned to read the whole Bible in about three days, but three months later I was still early in Matthew's Gospel (chapter 5) and struggling with everything Jesus said. One night I got so angry that I threw my Bible under the bed.

I vowed, "I am done with this book." Then I went to sleep. The next morning when I woke up, I felt an irresistible urge to read the Bible and get some closure: Is this book true or not?

I crawled under my bed and retrieved my Bible.

I started reading again, and I realized that all my confusion about life, spirituality, God, and religion, came down to one question: Who is this Jesus?

I struggled with the meaning of each verse in Matthew's Gospel. Before I had started reading the Bible, I believed that all religions were basically the same. They may look different on the outside, but if you study them like a research scientist, they converge into one truth.

However, after a few months of studying the Bible and comparing it to the Quran, I concluded that all religions are *not* the same. Although they look similar on the outside, if you study them deeply, you will see that they diverge, rather than converge.

The more I studied the Bible, the more it was evident to me that the Quran and the Bible could not both be true. Instead of finding answers to my questions, I was adding new questions to my list daily. And the ultimate question was this: Is the Bible true, or is the Quran true? Because both of them cannot be true!

A DATE FOR DIVORCE

Meanwhile, Donnell and I were even closer to the brink of divorce. We had virtually no relationship with one another. We talked very little.

Ironically, I had Donnell to thank for the Bible I had been studying.

She had come home after a late night at work to find me reading the Quran. I asked her if she still had a copy of the Bible that I could read. She said, "Yes." Thanks to her, I was able to read the Bible and encounter Jesus.

But that didn't signal an immediate improvement in our marriage. Most nights, Donnell came home late from work to avoid being at home with me. During these late nights at work, the janitor, who was from

Guatemala, would come in and collect the garbage from her office and see this sad woman working late.

He felt compassion for Donnell. He would bring her coffee and sometimes food from his home. They didn't speak much, because he knew only Spanish.

However, one night he approached Donnell to share a sentence he had learned just for her: "Jesus loves you."

It's amazing when I think about it. Donnell and I were both encountering Jesus. He was working on both of our hearts. I was throwing my Bible, and Donnell was getting Spanish lessons.

One night, Donnell came home from work to find me intensely studying and taking notes. She asked me what I was doing.

I told her, "I am comparing the Quran and the Bible. They're so different. I am trying to find answers. As a researcher with an analytical mind, having unanswered questions is true torture to me."

That's when she told me about the janitor and how he had insisted she come to church with him.

I said, "Okay, let's go. Maybe I will find some answers there."

We decided to accept the janitor's invitation to attend the Church of the Open Door in downtown Los Angeles, a church that provided services in English and Spanish. There, I heard the Gospel and realized how simple the message of salvation was: God loves you. You are a sinner and can never reach Him. But, because God loves you, He reached out to you through Jesus.

There, I heard the Gospel and realized how simple the message of salvation was: God loves you. You are a sinner and can never reach Him. But, because God loves you, He reached out to you through Jesus.

Donnell came to Christ on the first visit. Two weeks later, I prayed a simple prayer and invited Jesus into my life.

Instantly, I felt God's presence. And even more amazing, I experienced peace and joy for the first time. And this was not a one-time experience. I felt His peace and joy *continually.* I was changing from the inside out!

I was very excited to share this newfound faith with anyone I met, including my family, who were still in Iran. I wanted them to know that salvation is real. It works.

What's more, knowing God, experiencing His presence, and being changed by His transforming power were not complicated. You did not need to be an intellectual with an advanced degree to understand it. Even a child can understand it. That simple message changed me and my wife. It saved our marriage. Sometimes, when I challenge people for evangelism, I say, "The janitor at Donnell's company, who didn't speak English, led her to Christ. So, what's your excuse for not sharing the Gospel?"

While Donnell and I both found Christ, our marriage didn't improve overnight. We had so many problems that divorce still seemed like the best option.

However, while reading through the Bible, I came across Malachi 2:16, which states that God hates divorce. I shared this Scripture with Donnell.

We decided to wait, to obey the Bible, and give God a chance to work in our marriage. But it was very hard to reverse our decision to divorce. Neither of us could see any future for our marriage, even with God's help.

However, as we would discover later, God had plans for us, much bigger plans than we could even imagine.

We started attending English-speaking church services and Bible studies faithfully. Even though Farsi was my mother tongue, the language I was born into, English became my *spiritual* mother tongue. I learned how to pray in English and felt more comfortable connecting with God and worshiping Him in English than in Farsi.

When I understood that the Gospel's simple message has the power to change lives, save marriages, and transform societies, I felt a powerful mission growing inside of me: "If I don't share the Gospel, I am being selfish, because the Gospel is the answer to personal, familial, and even national problems. My wish is that every Christian would feel that way."

"YOU ARE AN INFIDEL!"

This season of my life marked the beginning of a new heart commitment I made to God: I would share the Gospel with others, even though it felt like torture to me. I was a shy, introverted scientist who felt very comfortable with books, but not with people. I preferred being alone to being around people, especially new people.

The Holy Spirit was telling me to share my faith, something that ran counter to my personality. Nevertheless, I pushed myself to share. With a rapid heartbeat and sweaty hands and a resistant spirit, I forced myself to talk to others about Christ.

I felt like a person who had been dying of cancer, only to be healed by a miraculous medicine. The "doctor" who gave me that medicine had given me a mission:

> "Go and share. I will give you an unlimited supply of this medicine. You will never run out. You have received this medicine freely, so freely give. The answer to personal problems, marriage problems, and social problems is all in this medicine!"

Before I began sharing with others, I asked the Lord one important question. "What about Islam?" I strongly felt that the Lord answered me by saying, "There is no salvation in Islam. It is a religion that has no power to change anybody. It is just a set of commands."

I was puzzled. After all, Iran had just become a powerful Islamic nation. But the Lord's answer filled my heart so powerfully. I believed, with every cell of my body, that someday soon Islam would be defeated in Iran. People would see its emptiness and be disillusioned. Then they would be hungry for true salvation through Jesus.

As I have confessed, I am a naturally shy person—probably shyer than anyone you know. But I forced myself to share my faith with Iranians in Orange County, California.

Most of them rejected my message and ridiculed me to my face.

Yes, God had transformed me inside, but I was still an introvert. I struggled to share my faith. It made me sweat. My hands became so sweaty and sticky that I would wipe them on my pants when I encountered someone new, just in case he or she wanted to shake hands.

On the positive side, I had been adventurous since childhood. I enjoyed trying new things, even if they scared me. Thus, I felt tortured when I shared my faith and tortured when I *didn't* share.

Because of this internal tension, communicating with others was an incredibly slow process. Whenever I shared my faith on the streets, distributed tracts, or spoke to a group of people, I wished I could speed up time. When the Holy Spirit prompted me to say something to someone, I immediately felt a bondage come over me. I knew it was all fear-based. Sometimes the fear won and I remained silent when I should have spoken. But sometimes I would speak up, despite my fear.

I was rejected and ridiculed many times by Iranians. The Islamic Revolution was still fresh in their minds. They believed that Islam was the answer, and that this faith would conquer the world. In these people's eyes, I had just made a big mistake by becoming a Christian. I needed to come back to Islam.

Others took a more extreme position: I was an infidel. They warned me that the fire of hell was waiting for me for betraying my religion and my country. Some accused me of being deceived, by Christians, into relinquishing my Iranian identity. To them, I had become Americanized.

I was crushed between the push of the Spirit and the push of the world against my beliefs and my personality.

I continued to feel those competing pressures to witness and to hold my tongue. Eventually, I forced myself to sign up for evangelism courses, such as Evangelism Explosion, which forced me to go door to door to share the Gospel.

I'll never forget February 11, 1981, the anniversary of the Iranian revolution. I was distributing tracts on the streets of Los Angeles.

Many people refused my tracts. Some even threw them on the ground after perusing them.

One man took the time to inform me, "You are an infidel who is betraying Islam and your people. You have betrayed our whole nation by becoming a Christian."

Then he warned me, "Islam is taking over the world." With that, he locked eyes with me, tore up my tract, and walked away.

I was shocked. But instead of being discouraged, I strongly felt God speaking to my heart, saying, "Don't be discouraged. Don't give up. Someday soon, I will destroy the honor and credibility of Islam in Iran, and many of these people will come to Christ."

ARE YOU DISCOURAGED IN YOUR FAITH?

During my early days as a Christian, converts were few and far between. I did meet a few other Iranian Christians in Orange County, and we decided to start a house church. It seemed like a great idea at the time.

For the next seven years, I started several house churches in Orange County and San Diego. None of them lasted long. I failed repeatedly as a church planter. I saw a few Muslims come to Christ, but I couldn't seem to help them form a strong house church. That task seemed beyond the abilities of an introverted research scientist.

One thing that kept me going was being on the radio. Shortly after my conversion to Christianity, I was contacted by Dick Papworth, an ex-missionary to Iran. He had just been kicked out of Iran, but he hoped to continue his radio broadcasts from outside the country. He invited me to be a radio announcer for Radio Voice of Christ, which targeted Farsi-speaking Iranians. (Radio Voice of Christ is now called Radio Mojdeh. Mojdeh means Good News.)

Being on the radio for six years, reading listeners' letters, and hearing their testimonies kept me on fire and motivated me to continue my efforts. It also showed me first-hand the power of media and prepared me to be a speaker and TV host later in my life.

Jeremiah 1:10 was a constant encouragement to me:

> "See, I have appointed you this day over the
> nations and over the kingdoms,
> To pluck up and to break down,
> To destroy and to overthrow,
> To build and to plant."

By God's grace, I never fell into Jeremiah's "I can't do it" attitude. I learned how to hunger for more, and my search for truth led me to Jesus. I knew He called me and enabled me. Still, this Jeremiah passage was daunting to me.

I knew I needed God's help to deny myself, pick up my cross, and follow Him if I wanted to be a world changer for Him.

I wanted to act with authority, but my personality, childhood experiences, and personal limitations held me back.

I was frustrated by my fears, and I felt I was falling short of my calling by failing to use my God-given, kingdom-building authority.

I knew I needed God's help to deny myself, pick up my cross, and follow Him if I wanted to be a world changer for Him. Then I remembered the morning I knelt beside my bed to pick up the Bible and continue my research. As Philippians 2:10-11 says,

> . . . so that at the name of Jesus every knee will bow,
> of those who are in heaven and on earth and under
> the earth, and that every tongue will confess that
> Jesus Christ is Lord, to the glory of God the Father.

I'm so glad I asked for God's help—and continue to ask for it—because I cannot do this life without Him. What about you?

CHAPTER 3

MY YOUNGER BROTHER WAS EXECUTED

MY MOM, SHAMSI, was a very intellectual person. She taught me the value of study and how to make the best decision based on knowledge. She taught me to never accept or reject anything without studying it. I started studying the Quran and the Bible based on her methods.

So, I thought she would be pleased to know that I had become a Christian after giving the matter careful study and thought. I was wrong.

My mother had a very sharp tongue, and she made her displeasure quite clear to me.

Then, when I was just a few months old in the Lord, I heard that the Islamic government had arrested my sixteen-year old brother, Hamraz, on some minor political charges. My brother was involved with the mujahideen, a group that was part of Khomeini's early regime, but was later destroyed by the ayatollah.

With my Mom focused on my brother's imprisonment, she became too busy to criticize my new faith. For two years, the Islamic government told my Mom that Hamraz was fine and doing his Islamic prayers in jail. He would be released soon, they promised.

But after Hamraz turned 18, my Mom received a call, instructing her to come to the jail to retrieve her son's body. He had been executed. She was even charged for the firing-squad bullets that ended her son's life. They would not release his body until she paid the cost of them killing her son.

It is important to note that my brother was never formally charged with a crime. There was no trial, no verdict. One day, the government decided to execute my teenage brother, without due process or any warning to our family. (Hamraz was not alone in his fate. The government executed all of the people who took part in the September 27, 1981 mujahideen uprising, in which dissidents attacked the police and the revolutionary guard. All totaled, thousands of mujahideen were executed in the months and years following the 1981 revolt.)

When I first heard the news about my brother, I was shocked. For two years, I had faithfully prayed for Hamraz's release. Why hadn't God answered me?

As a new believer who was still learning to hear God's voice, I was devastated by my brother's death. I shut myself in my bedroom, where I cried, prayed, and questioned God.

"Why didn't You stop them?" I asked. "There is so much evil in this world. Why don't You do something about it?"

I felt His gentle answer immediately. God reminded me of a truth I had read in the Bible. I felt Him saying to me, "I know what you are going through. They unjustly killed my Son, Jesus, too. By the way, I *have done* something about this evil. I sent Jesus to die on the cross to bring the Good News of salvation to the world. I have done My part. Now it is your turn to do your part."

Over the next two days, I prayed many prayers like this: "Okay, Lord, I will do something about this. I will take revenge on those who killed my brother."

"*No!* Revenge is mine,"

"But Lord, I hate them."

"Haven't you read in the Bible that I want you to love your enemies and not hate them?

"But God, I am angry"

"If you are angry at somebody, you have committed murder in your heart"

I argued, "Can I at least curse and badmouth the Islamic government so I can feel better?"

I already knew His answer: "You cannot worship Me and curse others with the same mouth."

"So what can I do? What do You want me to do?"

God had to remind me of this truth: "The Islamic government is not your enemy. You have only one enemy. His name is Satan."

I realized that those Muslims who killed my brother were themselves victims and captives in the hands of Satan.

"Do not hate them." God told me. "You must love them and desire their salvation. By the way, do you want to get revenge on Satan?"

"Yes!" I answered enthusiastically. "How do I do that?"

"What hurts Satan the most is when people leave his kingdom of darkness and enter the kingdom of light. When one gets saved, there is rejoicing in heaven and mourning in the courts of Satan, because he loses one of his slaves, his victims. If you want to hurt Satan really bad and get revenge on him, evangelize."

That is when I confessed the burden I was carrying, the feeling that I couldn't forgive those who killed my brother. I asked God to help me love them and enable me to share the Gospel with others despite my limitations.

Then God led me to read 1 Peter 2:9:

> But you are A CHOSEN RACE, A ROYAL PRIESTHOOD, A HOLY NATION, A PEOPLE FOR God's OWN POSSESSION, so that you may proclaim the excellencies of Him who has called you out of darkness into His marvelous light. . . .

I prayed that God would use me to help one million Muslims to come to Christ during my lifetime.

This verse encouraged me so much. I recommitted my life to the Lord—I would never stop evangelizing and loving others. I dedicated my life to sharing the Gospel. I prayed that God would use me to help one million Muslims to come to Christ during my lifetime. But at the time, I had no idea how this goal could ever be accomplished.

ARE YOU BOLD AND COURAGEOUS?

I knew I needed to approach my mother again and share this message of love with her. She had become very bitter against religion and God. After Hamraz was murdered, she completely renounced religion. She said, "There is no God."

When I talked to her about Christ, she mocked me. She told me I was stupid, despite my education and advanced degrees. Why would I fall for this nonsense?

She hurled sharp words at me, saying if God were real, He wouldn't have taken her son from her. All religions are man-made, she asserted, and used to enslave other humans.

When I tried to tell her about the words the Lord spoke to my heart while I was crying and praying in my bedroom, she wouldn't listen. She continued to call me regularly to denigrate and discourage me.

Fortunately, I had memorized Joshua 1:7-8 early in my Christian life. I replayed it in my mind many times, on many occasions. It says:

> "Only be strong and very courageous; be careful to do according to all the law which Moses My servant commanded you; do not turn from it to the right or to the left, so that you may have success wherever you go. This book of the law shall not depart from your mouth, but you shall mediate on it day and night, so that you may be careful to do according to all that is written in it; for then you will make your way prosperous, and then you will have success."

I never doubted that if I step out in faith and obedience to God, He will open doors supernaturally and help me. Another verse that helped to comfort me after my brother's death (and throughout many crises in my life) is Genesis 50:20:

> "As for you, you meant evil against me, but God meant it for good in order to bring about this present result, to preserve many people alive."

I never doubted that if I step out in faith and obedience to God, He will open doors supernaturally and help me.

I could have easily become bitter after my brother's execution. Instead, his death impacted me so much that I dedicated my life to sharing the Good News.

I realize that some readers might think I will never realize my goal of reaching a million Muslims for Christ. I've had my doubts, especially during those seven early years of unfruitful ministry.

But I have always remembered God's promise to me: "I will discredit Islam in Iran. Millions will come to Jesus in Iran—soon."

As human beings, we don't want to experience betrayal, pain, or death. But we can either allow God to strengthen us to serve others and live an adventurous life that leads to eternity, or we can allow bitterness and fear to confine us to boring and fruitless lives.

I have made my decision. What about you?

CHAPTER 4

"I AM GIVING YOU THE HONOR TO JOIN ME"

I **WAS BROKE** after I got my master's degree (in electrical engineering from USC), so there was no way I could continue my education. I had to work before I started my Ph.D. program.

In the midst of a great economic downturn in 1981, the Lord provided a job with Rockwell Aerospace, Satellite Division in Seal Beach. I thank God every time I think of the man who hired me.

Steve Mercadante treated me like a son. He provided me more than a research job, which was a blessing in itself. He also allowed me to work flexible hours and helped me secure the company financial support I needed to pay for my Ph.D. courses.

So I went back to USC and earned my doctoral degree in Computer Engineering in the fall of 1986 so that I could write my dissertation on Artificial Intelligence. My degree led to a dream job, based in San Jose, California.

Donnell and I had hoped to move to Seattle, where we knew a few people, but God had other plans. I received no offers from Seattle companies, but two from San Jose.

And even though Seattle was our first choice, working in Silicon Valley, the cradle of research and technology, was exciting to me, even though Donnell and I didn't know a single person in northern California.

I had gone from being an immigrant struggling to find a job in the middle of an economic downturn to a Silicon Valley research scientist. It was a dream come true.

"Lord, use us to save Iran!"

Before we moved to San Jose, I prayed, "Thank You, God, for blessing me and giving me the desires of my heart. You saved me. I wanted to get a Ph.D. but couldn't. Then You brought me to a place where my boss was so protective and provided for me. He gave me so much freedom to work, and the company even paid for my tuition."

It was very hard for Steve Mercadante to let me go. But he knew my departure was inevitable. Rockwell would not be able to pay me a doctoral-level salary.

After we settled in San Jose, Donnell and I asked the Lord to bring Muslims across our path.

He answered our prayer.

One after another, we met Iranian Muslims and started sharing the Gospel with them. The Lord had already sown the seed in our hearts for the salvation of Iran. I remember praying for Iranian souls in our living room in San Jose. Donnell and I often prayed, "Lord, use us to save Iran!" After each prayer, we would look at each other with puzzlement, as if to say, "What did we just pray? There are only two of us. We don't even have a house group, let alone a church, and we are asking for the salvation of Iran?"

Of course, those prayers didn't originate with Donnell or me. The Holy Spirit was prompting us to pray. This was prayer of supernatural origin.

Iran wasn't commanding international press attention at the time, but we still felt that God was leading us to pray for awakening in that nation.

LEARNING BY FAILING

In failing at planting house churches in Southern California, Donnell and I learned valuable lessons.

For example, I knew I was gifted in some areas of ministry but needed substantial help in others. I was good at starting groups, evangelizing, and teaching, but I needed people with pastoral, administrative, and, (especially) discernment and wisdom gifts by my side.

The Lord led us to an Iranian couple who had recently come to Christ. They were new believers who were gifted in the areas we had just prayed about. Recognizing they were the right fit, I focused on teaching and discipling them. They were truly gifts from heaven. Soon, other new believers joined my discipleship class, and together we built a strong core leadership team, the kind of leadership a new church needs.

We served the Lord together for years. Today, those faithful men and women are pastors and elders at the Iranian Christian Church in Sunnyvale, California. The Lord blessed us with a spirit of unity and made us effective. The church grew to 120 people in about three years. Almost all in our congregation were Muslim-background believers (MBBs) who had come to Christ through our evangelistic efforts.

For me, life was going well. I had a rewarding and well-paying job that I loved, a job with flexible hours that let me serve the church effectively.

God had blessed me with two beautiful children, which gave me much joy and rest in the midst of the challenges at work. And, I was on my way to getting a bachelor's degree in Bible and Theology from San Jose Bible College (now William Jessup University).

The church I planted was growing, not failing like the ones in Southern California. We hired a full-time Assyrian Iranian pastor to lead our church. I was totally happy being a church elder.

Then, amid all the peace and contentment, the Lord called me to change the course of my life.

It was a day like so many others. I entered my beautiful corner office, with its lovely view of the Palo Alto hills.

I arrived a little late, around 10, because our house church meeting the night before had run long. I sat down and turned on my expensive computer to test some of my new research ideas. My computer was programmed to ring victory chimes and light up with computer-generated fireworks whenever I tried a new concept and it worked.

Conversely, if one of my theories didn't work, the computer made a "PAC-Man" defeat sound, like when the "ghosts" eat him.

"Do you want to get paid big money so you can play games for the rest of your life?"

Yes, scientific research had become a game that I loved to play every day. So that day, as I was doing research (aka playing), a joy filled my heart. I started thanking the Lord. I prayed:

Thank You Lord for every good thing You have brought into my life: my salvation, my family, a great and growing ministry, and a great job where I can set my own hours. Lord, I love this job. I come up with research ideas, get my budget approved for the year, and get money to do it. I even have two programmers with master's degrees to do the boring job of writing computer program codes for me. I just do the fun stuff. I get paid big money to play games."

As soon as I uttered those last words, I felt a strong voice in my heart. It was not audible, but it was so powerful that it overwhelmed every other sound and thought. It was crystal clear: "Do you want to get paid big money so you can play games for the rest of your life?"

At first, I was not sure if God had asked me that question or if it came from my own mind. However, over the next few months, the question continued to haunt me.

I felt the Lord calling me to focus on building His kingdom. I argued with Him many times. I said, "I *am* serving You now. The church is growing, and I am serving it with my time, talent, and money."

I reminded the Lord that "pastor" is not among my top three spiritual gifts. I knew I was not gifted as a pastor, so *why* was God calling me? I also argued that we already hired a pastor for our small church. We couldn't afford to support two people financially.

"I AM GIVING YOU THE HONOR OF JOINING ME"

Logically, I did not see any reason to make a change. I had a great job that I loved. I was a research scientist in my favorite field: artificial intelligence.

I was paid very well, and my family enjoyed a comfortable life.

Yes, I *loved* working at the Lockheed Artificial Intelligence Center (LAIC) located in the beautiful hills of Palo Alto. Moreover, the church I had started in my home was going very well. To top things off, the Lord had just added another beautiful daughter (our third child) to the Shariat family.

Then, through a series of events, the Lord patiently and graciously worked in my life to prepare me to serve a nation that

I am going to do a great work in Iran and change that nation forever. I am giving you the honor to be a part of it.

He had prepared for transformation. He gave me a chance to have a part in making "His-story."

But I continued to struggle with the idea of changing course in my life.

I questioned God continually:

"What if the church won't hire me? We don't have money. And, by the way, have you forgotten my failures in Southern California? I am not a gifted pastor."

The Lord was responded to my objections, saying, "I am not calling you to be a pastor forever. Just for a period of time. I am going to do a great work in Iran and change that nation forever. I am giving you the honor to be a part of it."

This message from the Lord grew stronger and clearer over the next few months—so much so that when the opportunity came to change the focus and direction of my life to advancing His Kingdom full-time, I did it joyfully.

That message from the Lord was clear and consistent over the course of two years: I had to make a change. I began looking for teaching jobs at universities. I reasoned, "If I teach, I will have more flexible hours and summers off. I can do this."

But no positions opened up for me.

I was knocking on doors, and, after a year and a half of hearing nothing, my boss called me into his office. He said, "You know, we have to make some budget cuts."

He continued, "We have to cut some projects. All the other projects are interconnected, but yours is separate, so it's easier to cut. We cannot fund it anymore. It was such an easy and clear decision, because the other projects involve big groups of people, but yours affects only two other people besides you."

I had just been told I was being laid off, yet my heart was filled with great joy. I felt released.

I told God, "You asked me to make this change. I couldn't do it on my own, so You did it for me."

For the next few weeks, my co-workers thought I was nuts and needed therapy. They asked me out to lunch to question me:

"What are you going to do?"

"Are you okay? You look so happy!"

They all knew I was a Christian, so I told them I felt God had something special waiting for me. Even though I didn't know what was going to happen, I felt God's hand on my life.

However, I had made a mistake by failing to share my struggles, my spiritual journey, and my sense of God's call on my life with our church elders.

So when I told them about "my calling" (after my layoff), they were shocked. At the time, our church had an Assyrian pastor and three elders including me. I told them that God was calling me to serve full-time. They didn't feel the same way. They were skeptical, believing I was interested in ministry mainly because I had just been laid off.

I told them, "No. This is not about me desperately seeking a job. I really feel God is calling me to be a pastor."

They turned me down, so I had to look for another way to answer my calling. With only three months of severance pay to rely on, I got busy with my job search. When I got a job offer, I told the elders of my church about it. I told them, "Now, I have a job, but still feel called to the ministry."

That's when they changed their minds about me.

They told me, "Financially, we have enough to pay the pastor and partially support you, but to raise the rest of your support, you need to start other churches in Northern California." (They were looking for a way to share the financial burden.)

This was welcome news to me. It was confirmation from God. I have always been more excited by starting new churches than by staying in one place, pastoring one church.

I knew in my heart that God was giving me the honor to join Him, to be part of something eternal, something of histori-cal proportions.

I knew in my heart that God was giving me the honor to join Him, to be part of something eternal, something of historical proportions. I also knew full well that I would have to adjust and shrink my lifestyle dramatically to live on a small pastoral salary.

The church agreed to provide half my salary. The other half would come from starting new churches. Even though these churches would be small, they could all contribute something.

During its first seven years, our church in Sunnyvale experienced growth that was unlike the seven years of failure I experienced in Southern California. All our efforts were flourishing. I was evangelizing on the streets and going door to door to witness. Many Iranian Muslims came to Christ.

WILL YOU SAY "YES" TO A DIFFERENT LIFE?

We don't do God a favor when we say yes to a different life. It's an honor to follow Him and join what He is doing. You may not feel that God has called you. I can assure you that He *has.*

You might not know your calling yet. God might call you to quit your job, change your profession, or change your location. He might also call you to stay where you are, stay in your profession, and join Him to transform things where you are right now.

May I ask you to discover your calling—if you don't know what it is? For what purpose has God created you? How has He designed you to accomplish that calling? Next, I encourage you to obey God in your calling, despite your emotions or circumstances. The only thing you can do is put your trust in God. He will work out your calling.

Maybe your calling is being a Mom and raising three children. Or maybe it's working in the government or being a businessperson in the private sector. The point is not the calling. The point is obedience.

The point is not the calling. The point is obedience.

I am reminded of John 15:16: "You did not choose Me but I chose you, and appointed you that you would go and bear fruit, and *that* your fruit would remain, so that whatever you ask of the Father in My name He may give to you." (See also 1 Peter 4:10, Ephesians 2:10, and Acts 26:19.)

It's easy to say yes to God when it doesn't cost you anything. I knew that I did not want to play games for the rest of my life, and I knew that I had recommitted my life to reach one million Muslims for Christ. Once I decided to quit my job, I felt His peace, but the change was not easy. What about you?

CHAPTER 5

GETTING KICKED OUT OF THE CHURCH I STARTED

EVERY TIME YOU want to do something for the Lord, you will face spiritual warfare. That is just a fact. The bigger the mission, the bigger the war you will need to fight. You must believe God's promises, stand firm in your faith, and praise the Lord before you will see victory.

Even though the Sunnyvale church was growing, conflict was brewing beneath the surface. I started experiencing a mysterious attack on my mind and a deep darkness in my soul.

The demonic mental battle became so severe that I could not concentrate. I struggled to focus when I conversed with people. I wasn't really hearing what was said to me; therefore, I was not able to carry on a conversation. I was going out of my mind, and I knew it.

I sought help, and one of my teachers at San Jose Bible College encouraged me to contact Neil T. Anderson's ministry and attend one of his Freedom in Christ conferences. I attended a conference in early 1994. I spent a full day in prayer with a pastor, as I sought to experience spiritual freedom. That prayer time freed me from the demonic attacks on my mind.

However, even though I was doing better, those unresolved conflicts, buried in the hearts of the congregation, eventually surfaced, seven years after the church started.

Our church split in mid-1994, and our full-time pastor left, taking half the congregation with him.

I stayed behind, with a congregation of unhealthy and wounded people. We were not united. Factions formed. One group wanted to assume control of the church, and they started holding meetings in parishioners' homes. Leaders of this group were trying to convince everyone that I was not fit to serve as a pastor.

The church seemed hopelessly fractured. I remember seeking counsel from a pastor over lunch one day. He asked me about the leaders who were trying to turn people against me. Then he challenged me: "So, you are telling me that the people who oppose you are stronger in leadership than you are?"

That was painful to hear, but I knew he was right. My leadership was weak. I didn't know how to deal with conflict; I avoided it at all costs.

About two years later, my opposition felt they had turned most of the congregation against me, so they called for a vote of no confidence in order to dismiss me.

A special meeting was held one Sunday after the church service. When the votes were counted, it was clear: The congregation did not want me to be their pastor anymore.

The few who supported me were devastated and in tears. I had every reason to be discouraged and crying too. I had started this church in my home. I toiled day and night for nine years and made many personal and professional sacrifices. And now my church had rejected me.

I was kicked out of the church I started.

I had given up my career and had accepted a small salary because I believed this church would grow to have a great impact for God's kingdom, but now I was expelled.

I could make no sense of what had happened, but God gave me supernatural peace. He assured me that this was not the end of my story.

So, when "the opposition group" gathered at a restaurant to celebrate their victory, the Lord told me to join the celebration.

At the restaurant, the group was joyful and laughing. Meanwhile, I was having a peaceful conversation with the Lord in my heart. He was giving me peace and comfort. He encouraged me to avoid becoming bitter and losing hope. And He kept me from responding negatively to what was going on around me.

When my hamburger arrived, I saw a little flag on top of it. I felt the Lord instruct me, "Take that flag as a keepsake. You may think that this is the worst day of your life, but, when you look back, you shall see that this was one of the best days of your life."

I have held onto that flag to this day. To me, it represents an apostolic gift the Lord has given me: No matter how bad a situation is, I believe that God has a bright future planned for me. He is always ready to do a new thing. Isaiah 43:19 assures us:

> "Behold, I will do something new,
> Now it will spring forth;
> Will you not be aware of it?
> I will even make a roadway in the wilderness,
> Rivers in the desert."

I have always felt that If I do my part by operating in love and obeying God's will, He will fulfill His promise and make things work together for good. (See Romans 8:28.)

I know that if I guard my heart and keep it clear from bitterness and wrong motives, the Lord will bless my life. I believe that when people betray or reject you, if you follow Proverbs 4:23 ("Watch over your heart with all diligence, for from it *flow* the springs of life"), then the Lord will be on your side.

Someday soon, you will be able to declare with Joseph: "As for you, you meant evil against me, *but* God meant it for good in order to bring about this present result, to preserve many people alive" (Genesis 50:20).

The only things that bothers me from my past are questions like "Why was I not more wise?" and "How could I have been a better leader?"

A CONFIRMATION VISION

After I was kicked out of the church, the Lord gave me the strength to talk to the elders and the opposition leaders of the church and ask them if I could stay as a member, even if they did not want me as their pastor. They agreed.

For the next few months, I continued to attend church and serve as a teacher. I even preached occasionally.

The opposition group was not happy with that. They wanted to take over the church completely and kick me out.

So they started a new campaign to discredit me as a Bible teacher and preacher. They said my teachings were false. Some even declared that I was demonized. One person reported having a dream, in which he saw snakes emerging from my belly. He shared this "confirmation dream" with the whole church.

During those difficult months, I felt God's supernatural grace covering me and giving me the confidence to cease my fruitless striving and know that He was with me. No matter what happened, His plans would come true for my life. As Psalm 46:10 says, "Cease striving and know that I am God; I will be exalted among the nations, I will be exalted in the earth."

Most of the time, I was confident of my calling that the Lord wanted to save Iran and somehow use me in San Jose. But there were times that I struggled and doubted if I had heard Him clearly.

After all, I had given my life to that church for nine years. Almost all of its members had come to know Christ in the church. I had left my career and struggled financially to support my family of five on a pastor's salary.

But God saw my struggles. One day as I was praying, He gave me a vision. I saw a waterfall. The Lord told me, "Go and stand under it."

I understood that this was the waterfall of troubles and the Lord wanted me to stand there and face reality, rather than run away.

Those whom I loved and served had all rejected me. But, every time I was tempted to quit, the Lord lifted me up and confirmed His calling on my life.

I remember one day in particular. I was deeply discouraged and ready to quit. I was praying and asking God for confirmation that He wanted me to quit. By His grace, He showed me another vision, one I will never forget.

This time I saw many hills. They were crowded with so many people that I couldn't see any ground beneath them. There were hundreds of thousands of people—maybe even one million.

The scene reminded me of the promise I made to the Lord to continue to share the Gospel until one million Muslims came to Christ.

The scene reminded me of the promise I made to the Lord to continue to share the Gospel until one million Muslims came to Christ.

People were standing there quietly, young and old, men and women. And they were staring at me. It seemed that I could look into their eyes and know what they were thinking. Those eyes were full of worry, concern, and expectation.

People were awaiting my decision, hoping I would choose the right option. They were speaking to me with their eyes, as if to say, "Your decision will impact our lives. If you make the right decisions and stay, we will all be blessed. But if you go, we all will be impacted negatively. Please, please, stand firm. Do not give up; please continue, for our sake."

Several months after that vision—with the hard and selfless work of our dear brother, Pastor Luke Yeghnazar (founder and president of the Eternal Life Agape Ministries and the founding pastor of the Iranian Church of Los Angeles—the conflict was finally resolved. The group who opposed me left the church, and I was reinstated as the pastor by unanimous vote of the members.

I had just become the pastor of a very wounded church. We had all endured two church splits and years of internal conflicts. People had seen division and factions quarreling with one another. They had experienced the devastating impact of pride and gossip.

Our church had no spiritual energy left. Everyone was sick and tired, disillusioned about their church and discouraged about their Christian faith. No one trusted each other because of all the lies, pride, and divisions. Their faith in Christ was damaged. Many were depressed, bitter, and angry about what had happened.

I asked the Lord for direction. He showed me that we needed new blood in the church. I knew that if a few new people were saved and added to the church, we would regain our hope for the future and a zeal for the lost. So I started teaching evangelism. I encouraged the church to go out and share the Gospel. However, the people were too wounded to do so.

So I made evangelism my personal mission.

I went out by myself and met people everywhere and at any time to share Christ. When new believers started attending the church, we found new hope for the future.

Additionally, I came to realize just how much church members needed healing and freedom from the bitterness and traumatic events of the past.

Having experienced a personal freedom and healing almost three years before, I spent two years (from 1996 to 1998) translating Neil T. Anderson's *Freedom in Christ* materials into Farsi and sharing them with almost every member of the church. It took six to ten hours of prayer for each person to find freedom in Christ. Many times, I invested an entire day of prayer and counseling with individual church members.

By 1998, the church was healed. There was a deep love and unity among members. People felt sick in their stomachs when they encountered any trace of pride, gossip, or divisive talk. A supernatural work of God started, and the church began to grow rapidly. The whole church environment changed. For almost two years, anyone who walked in got saved—sometimes even before the sermon. It was supernatural.

The old church members were healing, but it was the new members who were coming to Christ every week and bringing their friends and neighbors with them. The fellowship was awesome. Every week, at the end of my sermon, people lined up to pray with me to receive Christ.

I would issue an invitation, and everyone in the church would see new people responding. For two years, the congregation doubled every six to nine months. There was so much love, humility, and unity among believers. It felt like heaven on earth. This experience showed me what a healthy church looks like. I started training new leaders right away. By 2003, we were able to plant five more churches in Northern California.

ARE YOU FINISHED?

During this time of growth, I had an idea for the next phase of church growth, but the elders opposed my plans. I felt a great desire from the Lord to equip the members and release them into ministry. I proposed to hire a person who could help me do that, but the elders felt we should focus on visiting people in their homes, The new hired pastor, they asserted, should help with *that* effort.

I did not want to fight with the elders. And I knew I couldn't effect change without their support.

I felt boxed in. I could see the golden years of our church slipping into a spirit of stagnation. Although the church was growing, I knew it couldn't sustain lasting growth without a new plan. Because I couldn't do anything about it, I felt useless and hopeless.

I could see the church stagnating, and I could not do anything about it.

For almost two years, I prayed, "Lord, I am done. I did what I could. Now I am stuck, with no hope to lead this church to the point of health where it can impact Iran. I have done what I could. Now take me home."

Yes, I prayed for death almost daily.

Then, one night I had a dream that changed everything. In the dream, I was wearing a beautiful shiny black tuxedo. I was checking myself in front of a mirror to make sure everything was perfect—and it was. My hair, my bow tie, my tuxedo—everything was perfect. I was *very* happy and joyful because I knew I was about to rest in a beautiful coffin. I was going to die and be with Jesus. However, as I started leaving the room, an intense sorrow suddenly filled my heart.

Yes, I was going to see Jesus, but He was going to ask me, "Did you finish the mission I gave you?"

"No," I would say shamefully.

I was troubled. I knew my calling and God-given vision, but I hadn't fulfilled it. I wasn't finished. When I woke up, I felt forbidden by the Lord to ever pray that death prayer again!

As I reflect on that dream today, this verse comes to mind:

> "For we must all appear before the judgment seat of Christ, so that each one may be recompensed for his deeds in the body, according to what he has done, whether good or bad" (2 Corinthians 5:10).

Psalm 16 was another passage that encouraged me. This psalm was my meditation during the hardest days of my life and ministry. Reading and praying through each verse made me feel so close to the Lord.

Leadership is a lonely place. Especially during hard times, leaders feel very alone. Whenever I felt that the church, elders (or even Donnell) weren't with me, this psalm helped me get close to the Lord and to realize, "Lord, You are enough for me, and You're not finished with me yet.

I know I am not the only one who has experienced a dark night of the soul and desired to be taken to heaven in the midst of a crisis. I have experienced failure, and I know what it feels like to fear starting over.

However, when you feel like giving up and throwing in the towel (or the tuxedo), you are often on the verge of the greatest breakthrough. In the next chapter, I will share how the Lord opened a great door of ministry, right after I felt so hopeless that I wanted to give up on life. So, my beloved, don't give up now. God is not finished with you yet.

So, my beloved, don't give up now. God is not finished with you yet.

CHAPTER 6

OUR SWITCHBOARD LIT UP LIKE A CHRISTMAS TREE

DURING OUR SEASON of church growth in the late 1990s, we applied for and received a free half-hour broadcast slot once a week on a public cable TV channel in the San Francisco Bay area.

With my plans for the church being blocked and frustrated, I suddenly had a bigger vision and a bigger opportunity for service. Standing on a street corner, and armed with a second-hand camera, we started recording our show.

A bit of background here: From 1981 to 1986, I had worked as an announcer for the Radio Voice of Christ in Southern California. Being on the radio taught me how to speak publicly. God knew I would need this training before He called me to be a pastor and, later, an evangelist.

In 1999, Donnell and I were praying when we sensed the Lord saying, "Iran is ready. I am breaking the power of the Prince of Persia. In the year 2000, a new era of spiritual openness in Iran will start."

So we made plans to start a new mission organization that would work beyond our local church and seek other churches and ministries to help us transform Iran.

In January 2000, we started a ministry called International Antioch Ministries, because we felt that our church, like the New Testament church in Antioch, would be used by God to spread the Gospel worldwide. Later, we changed the name to Iran Alive Ministries to reflect our initial call to Iran and the Persian people. We contacted several commercial and political Iranian satellite channels, which were springing up in Los Angeles. We asked if they would sell us an hour of weekly airtime.

Initially, all of them rejected our offer. The political organizations said they wouldn't allow *any* religious programming, as a matter of policy. The commercial enterprises feared losing sponsors if they broadcast Christian content.

So we simply waited and prayed that God would open a door.

Then, right after the events of September 11, 2001, one of the channels contacted us, offering a weekly hour of airtime—on one condition: We must sign a one-year contract and pay upfront for the entire year.

We jumped at the opportunity, even though we had to borrow from our building fund to make the payment. Later, we discovered that the channel was about to go bankrupt; that was the reason for their change of heart. We had no idea what was at stake: our ministry and our money.

On December 1, 2001, we started our broadcast via satellite, reaching the Middle East and Europe. With great excitement, my co-pastor Kamil Navai and I began hosting a weekly outreach program.

OUR SWITCHBOARD LIT UP LIKE A CHRISTMAS TREE

From day one, we got phone calls from Iran. Most of the people were touched by our presentation of the Gospel, but some were mad. We were sometimes cursed out live on the air. (At the time, phones in Iran were not monitored by the government, as they are today, so people could call us and speak their mind without fear of consequences.)

Pastor Navai and I would present the Gospel and then open the phone lines. We answered listeners' questions and prayed with them to receive Christ.

The calls to our multi-line switchboard were not limited to broadcast times. We received calls day and night. It was not uncommon for me to receive a call in the middle of the night, lead someone to Christ, and then go back to bed.

Every time we hit the airwaves, that switchboard, with its blinking lights, lit up like a Christmas tree. Pastor Navai and I couldn't respond to all of the callers, so we asked for volunteers to sit in the control room and minister to the multitudes of spiritually hungry people we were reaching. During every broadcast, many people came to Christ.

One listener called in and reported, "My extended family, about thirty of us, and I get together to watch your program. We have discussed Christ among ourselves, and we have all decided to follow Him. We have purchased a speaker phone, and we are gathered in my living room. We want to know how to become Christians."

That day, one of our phone counselors led that entire family to Christ.

I have never taken this God-given ministry for granted. I can still remember hitting the Los Angeles streets in the early 1980s—and the torture of trying to reach even one Muslim for Christ.

In 1984, William McElwee Miller published his book *Ten Muslims Meet Christ*, an account of ten Muslims who came to Christ as a result of his 40 years of missionary work in Iran. Now, decades later, and with the help of satellite television, thirty people could be saved in one short phone conversation.

Given the success of the broadcast, we decided to increase our hours, gradually. By 2004, we were able to buy enough airtime to broadcast four hours a day on various secular Iranian stations. Partnerships with evangelist Sammy Tippit, best-selling author and speaker Joyce Meyer, and pastor and businessman Mani Erfan (founder of the Christ for Crescent Moon Ministries) made the growth possible.

We were on our way to raising the support and enlisting the TV partners needed to start a 24/7 Christian broadcast, which we would call Iranian Christian Television (ICTV).

Then, the Christian Broadcasting Network (CBN) found out about our ministry and decided to join our effort. CBN helped upgrade our equipment and expand our ministry even further.

In 2005, ICTV and CBN started the first 24/7 satellite TV channel in Farsi. CBN took care of the expenses, and we will always be grateful for what they did for God's kingdom. The partnership allowed us to broadcast for eight hours a day.

At this point, tens of thousands had come to Christ through us. Hundreds of underground house churches started in many Iranian cities. We had a specific call to transform Iran through transforming lives and planting underground house churches.

We needed many hours of broadcast time to implement the strategy the Lord gave us—a strategy comprising evangelism, discipleship, leadership training, and church planting.

However, as CBN expanded their programming capabilities, their need for our programming diminished. Therefore, it was understandable when they cut our broadcast hours in favor of other programs, which were a better fit with the CBN brand.

By 2010, we had been reduced to three hours of programming per week, plus a live broadcast on Sunday. We could not complain because they were paying for it and it was legally their channel.

In 2011, CBN decided to pull all our programs from their channel. I sent them the most grateful email I could manage. I thanked them for all they had done for us. I knew everything belonged to God, so this decision must have been from Him.

In my prayers, I started asking, "Lord, am I done with TV ministry, or do You want me to continue? I have given You my life as a gift, so if You do not want to use that gift, then You have every right to do so. I will not complain.

"But please tell me clearly. I did not become a TV host to satisfy my ego. I know that is vanity and foolishness. Even if I am a famous TV personality, I have to put it down and pass it to others before my time on earth comes to an end, which is not too far in the future. If you think I am done with TV ministry, I will accept it with a joyful heart and thanksgiving."

During the first eight months that we were off the air, Donnell and I prayed like this continually, and I felt the Lord's constant assurance.

God told us, "No, you are not done. I have prepared Iran as a nation for transformation, I have called and gifted you to be effective. I have given you a supernatural wisdom and strategy, and I have provided a tool called satellite TV so you can go into every home to impact lives for Me. Again, you are not done! My favor is still with you."

"Then why is this happening to me, to our ministry?" I prayed.

I heard God say, "Do not become bitter. It was I who told them to throw you out, because, like a baby eagle, I want you to fly toward your destiny. You could not fulfill your mission there. But now you are forced to start a new channel, and I want you to fulfill your mission through *that*."

This response troubled me. I have always believed in partnerships. Launching a new satellite channel on my own was not my first choice. So I contacted other Farsi Christian channels and offered to join with them.

They were not open to that partnership, for various reasons. By closing the doors, the Lord was pushing us to step out by faith and start a new channel.

By God's grace, one thing I have successfully done again and again is to protect my heart and not become bitter during times of rejection. I have always believed, "No matter what other people do, I am responsible for *my* heart, including my spiritual and emotional health."

"FLYING" TO DALLAS

After much prayer, I felt strongly that the Lord wanted us to leave California and go to Dallas to start a new 24/7 Christian Farsi channel.

When I shared this news, some of our major financial supporters told me that they did not think it was from God. It was not a wise decision, they warned me, and it would destroy our ministry. We did not have much support for our move.

I wasn't sure what to do. I felt strongly that the Lord was leading us away from California, but it seemed like every external force was opposing us. For example, two of our top three donors cut their support.

We have all heard spiritual advice like, "Walk by faith and not by sight" or "Step out in faith and walk on water—even if you know you could sink at any moment."

Of course, I *wanted* to take a leap of faith. I didn't want to disobey God's call on my life, a call to reach a million Muslims for Christ.

It was so much easier to stay in San Jose. After 25 years of ministry, the church was stable. It was doing well financially, and we had trained about 40 leaders who were helping with various ministries. I could have just coasted in life and ministry. Except that was not what the Lord wanted, and I would be clearly disobeying Him.

On the other hand, I was afraid to make such a high-risk move, to "fly like an eagle" to Dallas. I knew that if we failed, it would erase years of ministry, and damage my reputation. And what about my staff members, who trusted me and were willing to move to Dallas with me? Their lives could be ruined as well.

Ultimately, I had to obey the Lord's strong leadership and take that big step of faith. Some of my critics called me "unwise" and "proud," but, by now, I was used to criticisms and unfair accusations. The Lord had prepared me for the negativity.

When enemies oppose me, their efforts usually have the opposite of their intended effect. The opposition make me stronger, more determined to persevere. However, when criticism comes from people you love, people who have been major supporters, that is a different story. When someone you trust threatens to withhold support (financial and otherwise), you must double-check your plans and your motives. I needed to make sure I was truly hearing from the Lord.

I have never shared this publicly before, but it was during this transition that I was invited to speak at a church with Joel C. Rosenberg. A Christian woman, who was an executive at a large corporation heard me speak that day. She then wrote a check for one million donation, and sent it to us with a request that she would remain anonymous.

It is not lost on me that God called me to reach one million Muslims for Christ, and, just when I thought I was finished, our transition was almost fully funded!

We took that great step of faith and moved to Dallas in July 2011.

In January 2012, we started Iran Alive's Network 7 Channel, broadcasting around the clock in the Middle East, North Africa, and Europe.

Through our earlier ministry, we had amassed the names of tens of thousands who had come to Christ during the first ten years. And there were hundreds of thousands more people who had been touched by our programming. All were happy to see us back on the air.

By God's grace, we were able to set up a classy studio and resume speaking truth into people's lives and hearts.

ARE YOUR DREAMS JUST THE BEGINNING?

The journey and the transition were not easy, but there is a blessing in serving the Lord and taking risks. A favorite Bible verse assures us . . .

> "Therefore, since we have so great a cloud of witnesses surrounding us, let us also lay aside every encumbrance and the sin which so easily entangles us, and let us run with endurance the race that is set before us, fixing our eyes on Jesus, the author and perfecter of faith, who for the joy set before Him endured the cross, despising the shame, and has sat down at the right hand of the throne of God. For consider Him who has endured such hostility by sinners against Himself, so that you will not grow weary and lose heart" (Hebrews 12:1-3).

This passage has always been a guide for my life and ministry: I need to get rid of sin in my life. I need to seek freedom from bondages and whatever is holding me back.

We pray for partners of all kinds to join us to impact Iran, and to reach one million Muslims for Christ.

Just like Jesus, there is a calling on my life. Just like Jesus, there is suffering involved to fulfill that calling. Just like Jesus, I can actually rejoice in that suffering. I must not grow discouraged and give up when I face opposition. What people say should not slow me down or change my mind. I must be immune to the criticism of people.

God has graciously positioned Iran Alive Ministries to have a significant role in transforming Iran into a Christian country. He has revealed effective strategies to us, and we are so excited about our future and the future of Iran.

One thing we know: We cannot do it alone. God is using other ministries also to accomplish His purposes in Iran. We simply focus on doing our part faithfully and with excellence. We ask God for gifted preachers and teachers to join us. And we pray for Christian businessmen, government officials, media leaders, and gifted artists to join us in our efforts. We pray for partners of all kinds to join us to impact Iran, as well as reach one million Muslims for Christ.

"I am going to do a great work in Iran, and through Iran, and I am giving you the honor of joining Me."

We ask God to raise up prayer warriors who will stand in the gap with us and pray (just like Daniel) so that the answer to our prayers will not be hindered by the Prince of Persia.

We pray for supernaturally talented people to join us as we use the powerful tool called media to impact lives for Jesus.

And, as you are reading these words, I want you to know that I have been praying for *you.*

Maybe you are the answer to our prayers! If the Lord is pulling on your heart as you read this book, perhaps He is calling you, saying, "I am going to do a great work in Iran, and through Iran, and I am giving you the honor of joining Me."

This is our dream! (Please turn to Get Involved on page 244 if you want to connect with me personally about this.)

CHAPTER 7

SIXTY-FIVE FAMILY MEMBERS COME TO CHRIST

DOES IT ENCOURAGE you to know that I have been praying for you as I write this book? I pray because I believe that what God is doing to bring the members of my own family, the nation of Iran, and Muslims throughout the world to Christ is bigger than my personal call and journey.

I want you to know that I didn't set out to become a pastor, Bible teacher, or even an international media personality over satellite. Although God's favor is still on my life and people around the world continue to receive my teachings, I want to leave a legacy of faith for the next generation. This is very important to me.

From the beginning of my ministry, I always had a passion to train others for ministry. It always gave me great joy when I saw others grow spiritually and serve in their calling. One of my favorite Bible verses assures us, "For we are His workmanship, created in Christ Jesus for good works, which God prepared beforehand so that we would walk in them" (Ephesians 2:10).

The last time I counted, more than 65 of my family members have come to Christ.

I could not have followed God's call on my life without the people He brought into my life to pray and partner with me. It is because of these people that my mother came to Christ. The last time I counted, more than 65 of my family members have come to Christ.

Back in Chapter 3, I shared how my Mom had to pay for the cost of my brother's execution in Iran. Hamraz's death impacted her deeply. She became embittered against all religions in general and against God in particular, even though she used to be religious. In fact, she once taught the Quran as a primary school teacher at various schools in Tehran.

As I mentioned earlier, my mother pestered me continually over the phone (and in person) after I came to Christ. When she lived in Iran, she would visit me in the United States for two to eight weeks at a time. These visits were a big burden for Donnell and me because my Mom was abrasive, sharp-tongued, and critical.

Every time my Mom visited, I invited her to attend church with us. She declined almost every time, stating that going to church is a waste of her time.

However, she would occasionally give in if she knew I would be preaching

But even then she would say things like, "I will go walk the streets [during the service], because at least that way I will get some exercise."

My Mom knew I was on the radio in Iran, and, unbeknownst to me, she listened. She said those broadcasts were one of the things that helped her stay connected with me across the miles.

However, she emphasized that she listened because I was her son. She did not accept what I was saying.

My Mom visited Donnell and me occasionally over a period of about fifteen years. Gradually, her spirit softened, but I knew she still was not open to the Gospel message. So I didn't push her. But she could see my grief over her, and how much I wanted her to be saved.

When I would drop her off at the airport, she would see my sadness and try to comfort me. She would say, "Son, don't worry about me. I believe in Jesus."

But when she visited again (months later), I would ask her, "Do you still believe in Jesus?"

She would reply, "There's no God. Who is this Jesus? I don't believe in this nonsense, and neither should you."

This scene replayed time after time.

Upon her returns to Iran, my Mom would tell me she believed in Jesus. I knew she was lying to make me feel better. Occasionally, she would even tell me she was a Christian, but nothing really changed in her life.

Until one summer, when our church hosted a camp.

I told my Mom that Donnell and I would be away at a camp, so, if she didn't join us, she would be home alone. She said she preferred loneliness to a Christian gathering. I told her that we were going to the mountains, because I knew she loved nature. I also told her that she didn't have to attend any of the meetings. She could just enjoy nature. With that, she agreed to come along.

On the conference's first day, Mom didn't attend any meetings. On the second day, she attended a morning session, sitting in the back for a few minutes. She stuck around a bit longer for an evening session.

The next day (a Sunday), featured some guest speakers. I was scheduled to close the service and give a short Bible message, along with an invitation for those who experienced God to come forward and receive Christ as their Savior.

My Mom was among the four people who came forward and knelt down. I knelt with her and whispered in her ear, "Are you doing this for me?"

I will always remember her response: "No, son, this time it's for me!"

It's important to note that about a month before that summer conference, my Mom was very ill. She was in so much pain that she thought she was dying. That marked the first time she came to church with us. At church, a woman noticed my Mom sitting in a back room alone, in obvious pain. She asked if she could pray for her, and my Mom said, "Yes."

Immediately after the lady laid hands on my Mom and prayed for her, the pain stopped. It wasn't until Mom became a Christian that she was able to connect the dots and see that her healing that day was supernatural.

My Mom was 76 years old when she came to know Christ. The day after the conference, she asked me to pray with her, but she didn't wait for me to start! She started praying and forgiving everyone, including those who killed her son, my brother.

My Mom was transformed overnight. Two days later, I saw her calling everyone she knew she had harmed, insulted, or offended. She asked for forgiveness. Some of the people my Mom called tried to counsel her back to Islam; others thought she was trying to scam them or hurt them again. Most people didn't believe she was sincere. I understood the skepticism. Only Jesus can turn a negative, bitter, and abrasive person into a sweet person who suddenly asks everyone for forgiveness.

After she became a Christian, my once-critical Mom called me regularly to encourage me with Bible verses she had read for the first time. And she prayed for me. Every time, she affirmed that I was truly called by God and that I was doing the right thing. I should never give up. I like to say she pestered me before she pastored me!

BIBLE SMUGGLER MOM

My Mom began her Bible smuggling career shortly after she became a Christian.

She was returning to Iran after one of her U.S. visits, and I asked her to take some Bibles with her. She responded, "Son, you know what happens if they catch me at the airport? They'll kill me."

I assured her, "Mom, your salvation is guaranteed. The moment you die, you would be with Jesus, because Jesus set us free from death." That assurance gave her courage.

"Okay," she said. "Give me some Bibles."

My Mom was brave. At first, she smuggled a few Bibles at a time. Eventually, she took suitcases full of Bibles and videos of *The Jesus Film* (also known as, simply, *Jesus*) to distribute in Iran. Many of my family members came to Christ because of her. They saw her life transformed. They received her words because she wasn't bitter anymore. Like her, they wanted to be changed by Jesus.

People would come to her house to watch the video or hear Scripture. An intellectual, my Mom was worried about the visitors. What if someone asked a question she couldn't answer as a new

Christian. I told her to simply tell people what Jesus did for her. God would do the rest.

One of my favorite "Mom stories," involves my cousin Farhang. She gave one of those smuggled Bibles to Farhang, who read the whole thing and returned with many questions that my Mom couldn't answer.

"So how did you answer him?" I asked Mom. "What did you do?"

She answered, "Instead of trying to answer his questions, I yanked the Bible out of his hands and told him, 'You don't deserve this. I'm going to give this Bible to somebody else.'"

She had such confidence in Christ and the Bible that she did not want to leave it in the hands of someone who was not spiritually hungry. This was one example of the Gospel's power at work within her.

Another story features Mom's cousin Zari, who came to her house one day and said, "I have had a headache for the past two years, day and night. It is ruining my life. It has disabled me, and I am not able to do anything. I have seen many doctors and have spent so much money. I have tried everything, but nothing has helped me."

My Mom told Zari, "There is one thing you have not tried."

"What *one* thing?" Zari asked.

"Have you ever asked Jesus to heal you?"

"No, I have not."

My Mom confessed to me, "I didn't have the faith or the courage to pray for Zari. So I told her to put her own hand on her head and pray to Jesus myself."

"Then what happened?" I asked.

"Zari prayed a simple prayer: 'Jesus heal my headache.' Instantly she was healed."

"Wow! Really? What happened after that?" I asked.

"Zari got excited and put her faith in Jesus. She then went around and prayed for everyone who was sick."

Many miracles emerged from Zari's experience. Many family members and friends came to Christ because this woman had the faith to believe for healing.

Zari's husband was a well-educated man who was the governor of a province in Iran. He told Zari that he didn't believe in any religion, but it was okay for her to be a Christian—as long as she didn't talk to him about Jesus.

Six months later, Zari's husband suffered a severe ear infection. He took all kinds of antibiotics, but the infection worsened. A doctor told him that he would go deaf without an operation. The night before the operation, Zari asked if she could pray for her husband to be healed in Jesus's name.

He said, "Yes!"

The next day, the doctors couldn't find any reason to operate, and Zari's spouse was sent home. He became a Christian, putting his trust in the Jesus who healed him.

I could share many more stories like these. Jesus healed members of my family from a variety of illnesses, including cancer. And it was all because my Mom told her cousin, "Put your own hand on your head and ask Jesus to heal you."

DO YOU NEED HELP TO EVANGELIZE YOUR FAMILY?

When it comes to sharing the Good News of Christ with your family, remember that you are not alone.

Whether they are Muslim or not, and no matter what objections they have about Jesus, winning them to Christ is not by force or nagging, but through prayer, wisdom, and living a Christ-honoring life. Remember this verse: "The fruit of the righteous is a tree of life, and he who is wise wins souls" (Proverbs 11:30).

I know you might object, "Dr. Hormoz, you don't know my family. You don't know what they are like."

But I can assure you, "When you pray for your relatives and witness to them, don't think you're alone. Don't think you have to convert your relatives. God has His own ways. Share a little bit, pray a lot, and be an example to them."

God will supernaturally bring other people who will share the Gospel with your relatives. If you have a loved one who is not a believer and you want him or her to come to Christ, don't give up. When your heart grieves for them, don't give up. Turn that grief into prayers. We all have family members who don't believe in Jesus. Let's not give up on them."

The good news is that it is not all up to you to convert your family.

I also want you to know that when God called me to reach one million Muslims, I felt embarrassed, even ashamed. I doubted that I could reach even one of my family members. But, as the years have gone by, many of my relatives have come to Christ.

I share my Mom's testimony because it is so dramatic. But I have many other stories about how other family members came to Christ. The good news is that it is not all up to you to convert your family.

NO POSTAGE
NECESSARY
IF MAILED
IN THE
UNITED STATES

BUSINESS REPLY MAIL

FIRST-CLASS MAIL PERMIT NO. 2 MELISSA TX

POSTAGE WILL BE PAID BY ADDRESSEE

IRAN ALIVE MINISTRIES
PO BOX 518
MELISSA TX 75454-9908

PART II

IRAN WILL BE A CHRISTIAN NATION

CHAPTER 8

FOR THE BIBLE TELLS ME SO!

WHEN I SPOKE at the *Epicenter Conference*, hosted by best-selling author Joel C. Rosenberg, I asked the audience, "How many of you believe that Iran will become a Christian nation?" Very few people raised their hands.

You see, most Christians are very familiar with Ezekiel 38, which prophesies that many nations, including Persia (Iran), will unite and attack Israel, and therefore they will be judged. I could not blame the audience for not knowing about another key Scripture: Jeremiah 49:34–39.

I have discovered that even most prophecy scholars with published books are not aware of the great promise God has given to Iran in the Jeremiah passage. I told the audience, "It does not matter if you believe Iran will become a Christian country or not. It shall happen, for the Bible says so, and that settles it!"

"It does not matter if you believe Iran will become a Christian country or not. It shall happen, for the Bible says so, and that settles it!"

That was my comment to the ones who did not raise their hands at that wonderful conference on prophecy.

I know some readers will counter, "But Ezekiel's prophecy is about Persia, while Jeremiah 49 is about Elam."

I will talk about these prophecies later. For now, let's remember that both Persia and Elam are a part of modern-day Iran. So both prophecies are relevant when we talk about Iran's future.

There is no dispute about Iran being ancient Persia. As a matter of fact, it was called Persia for many centuries. Then, in 1935, Reza Shah, the Shah (King) of Iran changed its name to Iran, which means "the land of Aryans." The name was probably inspired by the rise of Aryans in Germany under Hitler. (Reza Shah, incidentally, led Iran from 1925 to 1941, when he was deposed during the Anglo-Soviet invasion of Iran.)

Not many people know that Persians are not Arabs. They are of the Indo-European race, often called "Aryans."

Ezekiel 38 talks about Persia's aligning with other nations to attack Israel. However, Jeremiah 49:34–39 is where we can read, in detail, about Iran's future, including its end-times destiny.

In the following chapters, I will focus on this latter prophecy. Ezekiel's prophecies have garnered much attention. Many prophecy scholars have written great books on that subject. Therefore, I will not go into details about that prophecy. Instead, I will discuss how it relates to the Jeremiah prophecy in 49:34–39. Here is that passage:

> 34 That which came as the word of the LORD to Jeremiah the prophet concerning Elam, at the beginning of the reign of Zedekiah king of Judah, saying:
>
> 35 "Thus says the LORD of hosts,
> 'Behold, I am going to break the bow of Elam,
> The finest of their might.
> 36 'I will bring upon Elam the four winds

From the four ends of heaven,
And will scatter them to all these winds;

And there will be no nation
To which the outcasts of Elam will not go.
37'So I will shatter Elam before their enemies
And before those who seek their lives;
And I will bring calamity upon them,
Even My fierce anger,' declares the LORD,
'And I will send out the sword after them
Until I have consumed them.
38'Then I will set My throne in Elam
And destroy out of it king and princes,'
Declares the LORD.
39'But it will come about in the last days
That I will restore the fortunes of Elam,'"
Declares the LORD.

Before we study these verses, which detail Elam's future, we must ask, "Where is Elam?" Otherwise, we might wrongly apply prophecy and miss the Lord's true intention.

IS ELAM REALLY CURRENT-DAY IRAN?

Self-delusion and twisting prophecies to say what you want them to say are temptations facing many of us. That's why I have questioned this passage's relevance to Iran, and I have concluded that the prophecy indeed applies. Consider these three factors:

1. The land of Elam is defined as the land "east of the Tigris River."[1] This river is currently at the border of Iran and Iraq. So "east of the Tigris" clearly falls within the borders of present-day Iran.
2. At times, Elam covered most of modern Iran. Elam as a nation has changed its size many times during its history. At times, it was a very small territory. At other times,

it comprised most of today's Iran. Archaeologists have discovered Elamite writings and monuments as far east as Persepolis, as well as the modern province of Shiraz (which lies about 500 miles south of Tehran).

3. Elam is a province in modern Iran, and its capital is also Elam. Near the city of Elam is Shush, a city formerly known as Susa. Today, if you travel to Susa, you can visit the tomb of the Old Testament prophet Daniel, as well as the remains of castles where Persian kings resided. Shush (or Susa) was one of their capitals for winter.[2]

Also, one should ask: If this prophecy does not apply to Iran, then which country or nation does it apply to? Iraq, perhaps? But only a small portion of Elam falls within Iraq's borders.

BUT AREN'T THESE PROPHECIES ALREADY FULFILLED?

We might be tempted to look at every prophecy and categorize it as a "future event." But there are hundreds of prophecies in the Bible that are already fulfilled. Of course, verse 39 is clearly a future event, as it will happen "in the last days."

One could say, "Verse 39 clearly refers to the end time, but there may be a big time gap between that and verses 34 through 38. These events may have *already* happened."

Those are valid points. I had similar concerns. However, after studying this passage's relevance to Iran, I concluded that most of the events prophesied in this passage are future events, things yet to happen.

Here are my reasons:

1. The magnitude of the events described in these verses (such as the dispersion of Elamites, their mass murder, and the establishment of the Lord's throne) is staggering. If any of

these prophecies had already been fulfilled, they would have surely been recorded by historians. Consider the following five points:

2. To this point in history, the people of Elam (Iran) have not faced the severe judgment and tribulation mentioned in verses 35-37. Yes, Elam has been invaded by various armies (including the Babylonians), but never to the extent and severity mentioned in these Scriptures.
3. The people of Elam (Iran) have not been scattered worldwide to the extent that "There will be no nation to which the outcasts of Elam will not go" (Jeremiah 49:36b).
4. At no time in history have Elam's (Iran's) people enjoyed such a revival that the Lord would say, "I did set My throne in Elam" (Jeremiah 49:38a).
5. Kings ruled Elam (Iran) for more than 2,700 years, until the Islamic revolution of 1979. The removal of its king is mentioned in verse 38, but that is a relatively recent development.
6. It is logical to think that, because only verse 39 refers to the "last days," there might be large time gap, even centuries, between the events of verses 35-38 (the war and the scattering of the people) and verse 39 (the people's return to the land). But this cannot be, because those who are scattered in verse 36 are the ones who will come back in verse 39. So the gap cannot be long. Remember that even the Jews, who were in captivity for seventy years, when given a chance to return to Jerusalem, declined the opportunity. Few of them returned. Most likely, the generation that is scattered is the one that will return. So it is reasonable to assume that the events in this passage will happen in a span of about forty years. Unlike Jews, who keep their national identity wherever they live, Iranians readily assimilate

into a host country. Looking at the second generation of Iranian immigrants, I know that very few of them want to return to Iran—except, perhaps, as tourists.

Like many other biblical prophecies, the fulfillment of these prophecies is progressive. That is, some prophecies are fulfilled on a smaller scale before reaching their ultimate fulfillment. As we will see in a verse-by-verse study of our passage, the fulfillment of many prophecies has already begun. Many of these events have happened on a small scale. They are happening in a larger scale now, and they will reach full scale in the future.

Like many other biblical prophecies, the fulfillment of these prophecies is progressive.

For example, the scattering of Iranians to the nations started right after the 1979 revolution, and this scattering is ongoing, progressive. The large exodus mentioned in verse 36 is still to come.

At the time of Jeremiah's prophecy, both Elam and Persia existed. Both were rather small and insignificant nations. Elam was subject to Assyria (2 Kings 18:11) until the Babylonians defeated them in 609 BC and took over their lands, including Elam. At the time of this prophecy, the Babylonian Empire was at its peak. It ruled Elam, Media, and many other provinces that later came to be known as Persia.

Persia did not become a world power until 536 BC, almost fifty years after Jeremiah's death (in 586 BC). I am sure this prophecy was a big surprise and hard for Jeremiah to digest. Was God really saying, "I will set My throne" in that insignificant land and rule that weak nation"?

Of course, to him this prophecy's being unlikely at the time of its revelation is another indication that it did not come from human reasoning. It was a divine revelation.

The Persian Empire ruled most of civilized world from 536 BC to 330 BC. It encompassed many nations, regions, and people groups. Elam was (and still is) a province of Persia (Ezra 4:9). Its capital was Susa, which is now called Shush, and is a part of Khuzestan province.

PROVINCES RULED BY THE PERSIAN EMPIRE

Today's Iran was called Persia for more than 2,500 years, when Reza Shah changed the country's name to Iran. As noted earlier, the name change was designed to set Iran apart from its Arab neighbors, emphasizing the European roots of the Persian people. (Remember, the word "Iran" literally means "The Land of Aryans.")

For centuries, Persia was much larger than today's Iran. In the 19th century, Russia and Great Britain took away parts of Persia, which included Azerbaijan, Georgia, and parts of Armenia, Afghanistan, Turkmenistan, and Pakistan. To this day, Tajiks and many Afghans consider themselves ethnically Persians. Farsi (the Persian language) is spoken in those countries.

From an ethnic viewpoint, the Persians who migrated from the north (Europe) (circa 3,000 BC) and the Medes, who lived in the area even earlier than that, are both from the lineage of Japheth, the son of Noah. Assyrians, Elamites, and Arabs come from the lineage of Shem, another son of Noah. Today, due to Persia's longtime dominance over the region, the word "Persian" refers to all the nations and ethnic groups that live in that region, regardless of their ethnic roots.

Persia and modern Iran include, and have always included, the land called Elam.

To summarize, Persia and modern Iran include, and have always included, the land called Elam. Therefore, any prophecy related to Elam must apply to Iran. There is no other way to interpret it.

DO YOU KNOW YOUR ROOTS?

Genealogies are taken seriously in the Bible, because they have spiritual significance. According to the Bible, sins affect four generations, but a blessing extends to a thousand generations (Exodus 20:5-6).

As Christians, we must be aware of our forefathers' sin, so that, by faith in Jesus, we can protect ourselves from its curse. But we should also know the blessings of our ancestors. We should ask, "How did the Lord bless our forefathers? What was their calling, and how were they gifted?"

I have two more questions for you:

1. How much do you know about your ancestry? Some people study their genealogy out of curiosity or for fun, but Christians do it for spiritual insights. When you identify a sin of your ancestors, consider if that sin a weak spot for you too. This will help you achieve a more focused and effective prayer life about the temptations you face.
2. How much do you know about the work of God's grace among your ancestors? What were their spiritual gifts? How did God use them? God might have graced you with some of the same spiritual gifts. You might have strengths you haven't discovered yet. And you might not yet fully appreciate the strength of your gifts.

Names and their meanings are spiritually significant in the Bible. A spiritual transaction took place when God changed Abram's name to Abraham (Genesis 17:5). When the name of Persia was changed to Iran, it had a spiritual impact. How about you?

CHAPTER 9

IRAN WILL BE ATTACKED

OVER THE NEXT few chapters, we will study Jeremiah 49:34–39, so let's review what it says:

34 That which came as the word of the Lord *to Jeremiah the prophet concerning Elam, at the beginning of the reign of Zedekiah king of Judah, saying:*

35 "Thus says the Lord *of hosts,*
'Behold, I am going to break the bow of Elam,
The finest of their might.

36 'I will bring upon Elam the four winds
From the four ends of heaven,
And will scatter them to all these winds;
And there will be no nation
To which the outcasts of Elam will not go.
37 'So I will shatter Elam before their enemies
And before those who seek their lives;
And I will bring calamity upon them,
Even My fierce anger,' declares the Lord,

'And I will send out the sword after them
Until I have consumed them.

38 'Then I will set My throne in Elam
And destroy out of it king and princes,'
Declares the Lord.

39 'But it will come about in the last days
That I will restore the fortunes of Elam,'"
Declares the Lord.

SHOULD WE INTERPRET THIS PASSAGE LITERALLY OR SPIRITUALLY?

Should we approach Jeremiah 49:34-39 purely as a prediction of historical events, or should we look at it spiritually? Are the battles mentioned physical or spiritual? The answer, as evident in the text, is both.

It is clearly a description of a physical war, as the passage mentions that Iran will be attacked from four sides and that Iran's people will scatter to all nations. Many will die. But the passage also describes a spiritual battle. We see that the Lord will remove the king and princes. Then God will establish His throne and rule in Iran.

In our spiritual lives, we must achieve victory in the spiritual domain before we see impact in the physical domain.

God's kingdom is never only physical; it's always spiritual too. Because God will rule Iran, His battle will be against the country's dark spiritual rulers *and* its political rulers. He will achieve victory on both fronts. The heavenly and earthly realms are always connected and interacting with each other.

That is why faith and prayer are so powerful. In our spiritual lives, we must achieve victory in the spiritual domain before we see impact in the physical domain. No wonder that binding things in heaven and on earth is so connected (Matthew 18:18). Early in our Jeremiah passage, God introduces Himself as the Lord of hosts (heavenly armies).

Now, let us dive into our verse-by-verse study of Jeremiah 49:34–35.

JEREMIAH 49:34

"That which came as the word of the LORD to Jeremiah the prophet concerning Elam, at the beginning of the reign of Zedekiah king of Judah, saying. . . ."

This verse establishes background for what follows. First, we know that this word comes directly from the Lord. The body of the prophecy emphasizes this point, as the Lord speaks in the first person:

"Concerning Elam"—The word "concerning" is rendered "against" in the King James Version. However, that word does not exist in the original language. The Hebrew word that appears there is 'El,' which is a common word, usually translated as 'to' or 'unto' elsewhere in the Old Testament. All other translations correctly have chosen "concerning Elam" or "about Elam" instead.

However, it is understandable why the translators of the King James chose *against.* There are indeed severe judgments and calamities prophesied for Iran in these verses. Most of these verses are truly prophecies *against* Iran.

"At the beginning of the reign of Zedekiah king of Judah"—King Zedekiah started his rule in 597 BC, about ten years before Jerusalem fell to the Babylonian army. Elam was a part of the Babylonian Empire at that time, and Elamite soldiers were probably part of the army that attacked Jerusalem. More on this later.

JEREMIAH 49:35

"Thus says the LORD of hosts, 'Behold, I am going to break the bow of Elam, the finest of their might."

Here, the Lord of hosts (heavenly armies) declares war against Iran. This war has physical and spiritual dimensions. Before Iran becomes a Christian nation and God's throne and rule are established, there will be a time of destruction. There will be a time of breaking down before a time of building. There will be a time of suffering before a great time of blessings (Ecclesiastes 3:1-8).

Iran's people have been suffering a lot. They will suffer even more before God's promise for blessing is fulfilled. Today, they are enduring great calamity in every area of their lives, and they see no end to it. They cannot speak up or complain. When they do, they face bullets.

God is breaking the pride and the will of Iranians to humble them, so that He can bless them. He is allowing them to be desperate so they will seek Him. He is allowing them to be hopeless so that He will be their only hope. This suffering will precede a great revival.

Isn't this a spiritual principle that we see throughout the Bible? The Lord allows suffering to make us humble, so that we qualify for His grace. Then, through His grace, He lifts us up and blesses us. Life's great blessings usually come through great suffering. The Lord allows our hearts to be broken so that we can see our desperate need for Him. When people betray us and let us down, He uses that to free us from the curse of trusting humanity. Then we can receive the blessing of trusting Him (Jeremiah 17:5).

The Lord allows suffering to make us humble, so that we qualify for His grace. Then, through His grace, He lifts us up and blesses us.

Through brokenness, we experience a new and deeper intimacy with God

(Psalm 34:18). Through brokenness, we can view life through fresh eyes—the eyes of our Lord. We understand what is important in life and what is not. We understand and care about the suffering of other people.

That is why a persecuted and suffering church is a strong church. When there is no persecution, when the church is free and prosperous, it becomes weak. It struggles with complacency and mediocrity. But a persecuted church can be vibrant and powerful, so powerful that it can change a nation and even the world. That is what the first-century church did, despite severe persecution by religious and political leaders. That is what is happening to the persecuted church in Iran, China, and other countries.

When suffering and calamity come to a nation, that nation can be transformed. Hardship can cause a nation to be broken and humbled humbled, so it might fall might fall on its face and seek the Lord. This can cause a nation to enter a new level of intimacy with and surrender to the Lord.

When suffering and calamity come to a nation, that nation can be transformed.

This is what we saw (briefly) in the United States right after the events of September 11, 2001. I do not want to minimize this tragedy, but it was one event in one day. That is why the spiritual awakening afterward was so short-lived. What would have happened if that attack targeted all US cities and lasted for many years? What if it was so severe that people would rather leave everything and flee to Mexico or Canada—and be killed by the millions as they were fleeing? A horrible picture, isn't it?

If that had happened, then the spiritual spark that was ignited in the hearts of Americans after 9/11 would have not died so quickly. It would have become a spiritual fire that would have transformed the United States into the world's most spiritual country.

As a result, Iranians will turn to Christ in such large numbers and with such deep commitment that it will be unprecedented in history. It probably will surpass all the revivals in history.

This is exactly what we will see in Iran. According to Jeremiah 49:34–49, Iran will go through an unthinkable period of adversity, hardship, and tribulation. As a result, Iranians will turn to Christ in such large numbers and with such deep commitment that it will be unprecedented in history. It probably will surpass all the revivals in history. There have been many revivals that brought major changes in various societies. Some were local and some worldwide. But none of them had such an impact that the Lord could say:

"I rule here. I have set My throne here. These people love and worship Me as their King and obey Me in every area of their lives. I am ruling their hearts, and I am ruling their society. I can do what I want to do because they obey Me. They have My mind and My heart. They do My will."

So Iran will go through such total transformation that God will say, "I have set my throne there."

"Thus says the LORD of hosts"—Before proclaiming some verses loaded with military language, Jehovah introduces Himself as the Lord of the heavenly armies.

It seems that He is saying, "I am going to declare My judgments. It will look like earthly forces are attacking Iran. You may look at events and think, 'Where is God?' It is going to be bad, very bad. But I tell you that My heavenly armies and I are involved. You may see the physical battle, but there will also be a spiritual battle going on in the heavenlies, something you will not be able to see at first. In the end, you will see the result. You will come to know Me. You will receive My salvation. You will be changed. You will be Mine. I will be your King, and you will be My people. "My beloved, things may look really bad around you for a while. It may look like you are being defeated and destroyed. On earth, it will look like I am fighting against you, but in the heavenly domain I am fighting for you with My army. I am winning a great spiritual victory for you. Just wait and see. The end will be not good, but great."

It is interesting that the first word the Lord says is, "Behold" (*hin-nay* in Hebrew). The word means "pay attention" or "look carefully." Before declaring unsettling judgments and prophesying hard days for Iranians, He assures them. He tells them, "Be observant and know I will bring the following events to pass. If you don't look carefully, you may get entangled with the horrendous events and sufferings of the moment and fail to realize that all was initiated by Me. I am still in control."

It is like a father telling his sick child who needs an operation, "There will be an operation. It will be painful, but I will allow a doctor, whom you might think is your enemy, to operate on you. But don't forget that I will take you to the operating room. I love you and promise to be with you throughout the operation. In the end, you will be so healthy, like never before."

So, by saying "pay attention", the Lord is directing us to avoid looking at the following verses only as earthly events of historical importance. He wants us to regard them as a war in the heavens, with eternal spiritual importance. Therefore, that is how we will interpret the following verses.

"I am going to break the bow of Elam"—The word 'break' here is the Hebrew *shabar*, which means "to smash, shatter, and break to pieces." It is the same word used in Exodus 32:19, where Moses shatters the stone tablets at the foot of the mountain. But what is "the bow of Elam?"

Is there a bow for the whole country? Some Bible scholars of the past (who did not live to see the recent events happening in the world and in Iran) tried to make sense of this. They referred to Isaiah 22:6, which reads, "Elam took up the quiver with the chariots, infantry and horsemen; And Kir uncovered the shield."

From this verse, they concluded that because Elamites were carrying the quiver in the war against the Israel, the Lord judged them and punished them. But remember that at the time of this Assyrian attack on Israel (when Isaiah 22:6 was written), Elam was a weak and subdued nation. As mercenaries, they composed only a fraction of Assyria's large army.

Others claim this prophecy was fulfilled when the Babylonians defeated the Assyrian kingdom in 609 BC. But this interpretation is questionable. For example, the judgment described in Jeremiah 49 is so severe and sweeping that it doesn't match Elam's small role in assisting the Assyrian army. (See Isaiah 22:6.) And historical records don't depict the Elamites ever suffering such severe judgment.

As we will see later, however, Iranians will be involved in a major offense that *will* warrant this level of divine punishment.

WHAT IS "THE BOW OF ELAM?"

First, note that the word "bow" is singular, and it refers to the whole nation. And what is a bow? A bow launches arrows, of course. In modern-day warfare, the arrows are missiles, so a bow is where these missiles are launched. It's a missile launching base.

In addition to developing nuclear programs, Iran's government has invested a large amount of money and resources in developing long-range missiles. They have missiles like the Shahab 3 (or Shooting Star 3), with a reach of 2,000 kilometers (or 1,243 miles).

These missiles can reach Israel in seven minutes. Israel is about 1,000 kilometers (600 miles) away from Iran's western borders. The US military bases in the Middle East will also be within reach, and they are high-value targets for Iranian missiles.

Another missile, the Shahab 4, is used to launch satellites into orbit. And Shahab 5 is a missile with a range of over 4,000 kilometers (about 2,500 miles). It can reach London. Shahab 6 is an intercontinental ballistic missile (ICBM) with a range of more than 10,000 kilometers (about 6,200 miles). The Shahab 6 could reach New York.

The US. Navy's Fifth Fleet is based in Bahrain, some 200 kilometers (120 miles) from Iranian shores in the Persian Gulf. It will be one of the first targets when a war breaks out.

From ancient times, Iranians have been extremely skilled archers. The Greek historian Strabo noted their prowess, while Herodotus mentions the "uncommon size" of Elamite bows. Modern Iranians are continuing the tradition. They are adept at today's version of archery: building and launching missiles.

So it makes sense that in the upcoming war against Iran, its missile bases will be attacked first. Attacking missile sites is a standard tactic of modern warfare. And it was predicted by Jeremiah 2,600 years ago.

From a political perspective, the bow also is the source of orders for attacks. In Iran, the source of political power is not vested in the president or the parliament (Majlis).

Instead, the ultimate political power rests in the hands of the Supreme Leader. Could this mean that his residence will be attacked, along with the missile sites? I believe this is a reasonable assumption, a likely scenario.

"The finest of their might"—This phrase can be translated as "the source of its power." The word "finest" ("chief" in KJV) is the Hebrew term *reshiyth.* This

This word has the honor of being the first word in the Bible. Genesis 1:1 starts with the word bereshith, translated as "In the beginning."

word has the honor of being the first word in the Bible. Genesis 1:1 starts with the word *bereshith*, translated as "In the beginning."

The word is used in many other places in the Old Testament, often indicating the idea of "first" or "foundational." In Proverbs 1:7, we read, "The fear of the Lord is the beginning (*reshiyth*) of knowledge. Fools despise wisdom and instruction." In other words, the fear of the Lord is the source and foundation of knowledge and wisdom.

Using the same word (*reshiyth*), in Jeremiah 49:35, the Lord promises to destroy Iran's foundation and source of power. In other words, He will shatter and annihilate what makes Iran powerful.

HOW WILL THE LORD BREAK "THE BOW OF ELAM?"

What makes Iran powerful, and how the Lord will destroy Iran's power bases? The Iranian Government has the following four bases of power. So one or all of them could be attacked if a war breaks out.

1. *The Base of Military Power:* Nuclear Bombs.

At the time of the war prophesied in Jeremiah 49, Iran will probably have a nuclear bomb. So, it is likely that its nuclear bases will be attacked early in the war. In fact, Iranian lawmaker Ahmad Hamzah said recently, "If we had nuclear weapons today, we would be protected from threats. We should put the production of long-range missiles capable of carrying unconventional warheads on our agenda. This is our natural right."[3]

Those doubting that the Iranian government is vigorously pursuing the development of nuclear bombs must answer some hard questions:

> Why would Iran's government spend billions of dollars over the years to develop long-range missiles? To deliver what? Persian pistachios? Or nuclear bombs?

Developing those long-range missiles and intercontinental ballistic missiles (ICBMs) doesn't make sense unless a nuclear payload is also being developed.

To understand the situation in Iran, one must realize that the government has total power and control over its people. It has exerted its power with so much violence that Iranians live under constant fear and intimidation. Even the slightest political movements and protests are crushed ruthlessly. Any opposition to or criticism of the government results in long prison sentences and even execution.

The Islamic Republic of Iran has systematically eliminated its opposition. Even moderate clergy inside the government have been fired, arrested, or punished in other ways. The government has so much control that the people lack the hope and courage to stand up to oppression. People know they will pay a high price if they want to topple the government. If they are not willing to die, they can't make much of a difference.

To reinforce fear and impose its control, the government has killed emerging political figures who aren't even a threat yet, but who would pose a potential threat in the future.

Iran's government does not need nuclear weapons to control its people. Leaders are confident because they believe that their policies of violence and intimidation will control the people, now and in the years to come.

They do not see any challenge or threat from the Iranian people. What worries them (even scares them) is a military attack by the United States, Israel, and their allies. Such an attack could topple them. And, according to Jeremiah 49, an attack will happen.

Having a nuclear bomb benefits Iran in two major ways. First, it provides security against a foreign invasion. None of Iran's neighbors dare to attack them, and they don't want to be used as a base for an attack by another country. However, Iran's leaders *are* afraid that the United States Navy will attack them from the Persian Gulf.

They know their military is no match for America's, so they have stated several times, "No matter who attacks us, in response we will attack Israel with our long-range missiles, and with our proxy army, Hezbollah of Lebanon."

The second benefit? Iran's government can now threaten, intimidate, and bully other countries in the region. They can also threaten Israel and the United States. Their policy of fear and intimidation, which has served them well inside Iran, will go global. Iran can be the region's bully, imposing its will as it chooses.

Having a nuclear bomb is not just an insurance policy; it also promises a bright future of political dominance in the region.

For these reasons, Iran will never abandon the goal of making nuclear bombs. It's quite likely that Iran will purchase a nuclear bomb from North Korea and even detonate it in a desert inside Iran. Then they will falsely claim that they have built the weapon, and that they have many more, ready to use.[4]

The Iranian government has been belligerent, proud, and confrontational, even without a nuclear bomb. How much more will Iran show these attitudes when it does have a nuclear arsenal?

So, the prophecy in Jeremiah 49:35 could mean that Iran will have a nuclear bomb, which will be the source of its political might. And Iran will suffer an attack on its nuclear facilities and missile sites.

2. *The Base of Economic Power:* The Oil Wells

Iran's economy depends on its oil and gas. Because of sanctions and economic mismanagement, this is more true than ever. The oil and gas industry are totally owned and operated by the government. Its income directly fuels the government's existence and is used to implement its policies domestically and internationally.

The oil and gas industry have *not* helped build the country's infrastructure or expand its economy. Instead, the government uses these fuels to ensure its survival.

Oil and gas profits fund the Islamic Revolutionary Guard Corps (IRGC) and its many specialized sub-groups: secret police, phone control, and internet policing. Iran's cyber police are one of world's strongest and best-funded agencies. (During the early days of the coronavirus scare, the cyber police arrested 24 people for spreading rumors online and inciting panic.)

The cyber police have enough agents to monitor all political and non-Islamic religious chat rooms on the internet. (And there are, perhaps, thousands of these chat rooms.)

Iran Alive Ministries has online public chat rooms dedicated to evangelism. We have online classes to teach and equip Iran's Christians, and online churches to provide a sense of community to isolated believers. And we know that there is at least one government agent monitoring each chat room's activity. What's more, our chat rooms are often "invaded" by large groups of agents who try to take control.

And there are agents who have been trained to pretend to be Christians, and they infiltrate our online classes and Christian gatherings.

Iran's cyber police are well funded by oil money. They have the personnel and the technology to monitor citizens' activities. People have been arrested for visiting Christian or political sites. Moreover, visiting any of these organizations' Facebook pages is dangerous for an Iranian citizen. Merely "liking" a post can get you arrested.

There are many fake Facebook and Twitter accounts, as well as phony websites under my name or our ministry's name. Many Iranians who intended to contact us have actually connected with a fake social media outlet, resulting in their arrest. The problem persists, and Facebook and other social media companies have not been responsive to our efforts to correct the deception.

But even though the phone lines to our TV ministry are blocked in Iran and the internet is government-controlled, many people still find ways to contact us.

Meanwhile, the Iranian Cyber Army is one of the world's best funded and most sophisticated operations of its kind. Given Iran's 30-percent unemployment rate, many of the country's brightest, most talented, and best-educated young people cannot find jobs. So the government has the luxury of hiring the best of the best for the Cyber Army.

Most Christian websites (and other "opposition" websites) are attacked weekly, if not daily. The cyber police have shut down Twitter several times, because Iranian youth often use this platform to communicate with one another, and to inform the world about what is happening in their country.

The Cyber Army has repeatedly targeted the banks in the United States. The attacks have been so sophisticated that even big banks like Bank of America, JP Morgan Chase, Citibank, Wells Fargo, and Bancorp, have not been able to stop them. Even though these banks possess huge financial resources and stat-of-the-art security technology, they had to ask the United States government for help. One bank spent over $10 million to protect itself, and that was not enough.[5]

Internationally, the Iranian government has used oil and gas income to implement its foreign policy goals. The Islamic Republic's annual budget contains line items for assisting Hezbollah in Lebanon, Syrian President Bashar al-Assad, and Shiites in Iraq and Yemen. The goal is to bring all those countries under the rule of Shiite clergy.

More than once, the Israeli navy has intercepted arms deliveries to Hezbollah. Commercial ships and passenger airlines have been used to deliver weapons to Hezbollah in Lebanon, and military support to Syria.

According to *USA Today*, Iran's oil reserves rank fourth in the world,[6] while its gas reserves rank second.[7] Oil and gas revenues will play an important role in Iran's economy for years to come.

Therefore, a severe war, as described in Jeremiah 49:35-37, will certainly target Iranian oil and gas operations. Early in this war, we can expect attacks on major oil fields, refineries, ports, and, especially, the pipelines for oil and gas sales.

3. *The Base of Political Power:* The Supreme Leader and the Top Clergy

Iran is the only country in the world ruled by clergy. Iran's laws are based on Sharia, the Islamic laws. In 1979, Iranians hoped for democracy when they rallied behind Khomeini to topple the dictatorial ruler Mohammad Reza Shah also known as Mohammad Reza Shah Pahlavi. However, this was an "anti-Shah" revolution, not a "pro-Islam" revolution.

The revolution resulted in a strict, brutal, and oppressive form of religious dictatorship. Now the leadership had God on their side (or so they thought). Thus, enemies of the government were viewed as enemies of God. The government could pass judgment and issue death penalties, under mandate from Allah.

On the surface, today's Iran looks like a democracy. The people elect the president and the members of congress—called Majlis—every four years.

However, the ultimate power rests with the Supreme Leader first and foremost, and then with the Council of Guardians. (This council comprises a group of top clergy who oversee all government functions, policies, and laws.) The council vets candidates before every election, and only those who have a track record of submitting to the Supreme Leader appear on the ballot.

Despite this filtering of candidates, the "elected" officials hold no real power. Today, Supreme Leader Khamenei must approve every decision the president or congress makes before it is accepted as law and implemented. He has veto power on all decisions.

The main responsibility of all elected officials is to implement the Supreme Leader's policies. Even though they are "elected" by the people, they don't serve the people. They serve the wishes of the Supreme Leader and his associates.

Thus, the coming war will also target the Supreme Leader himself. In recent history, we have seen this tactic as a first step of war, or even a precursor to war.

For example, Saddam Hussein's residence was attacked in 1991, at the beginning of Operation Desert Storm, and again in 2003.

And in 2011, Libyan leader Moammar Gaddafi's villa was attacked (via a NATO air strike), and one of his sons was killed.

Iran's top clergy reside in the city of Qom, which could be called the "Vatican of Shiite Islam." The Ayatollah Khomeini, the founder of the Islamic Republic of Iran, once lived in Jamaran, a town on the outskirts of Qom. Ali Khamenei lives in the heart of Tehran.

So, to recap, in the early stages of the war described in Jeremiah 49:35-37, the Supreme Leader's residence and the city of Qom will be targeted.

4. *The Base of Spiritual Power:* Islam

In Daniel 10:13, we read that a powerful dark angel resides over Persia (Iran). (Remember, at that time, Persia was an empire with Elam as one of its provinces.) This dark spirit, called the prince of Persia, holds the high rank of "prince of darkness." In the same verse, the Archangel Michael is called "one of the chief princes."

Therefore, in spiritual ranking, the prince of Persia is equal to Michael. Yes, the Bible warns us that a high-ranking dark spirit rules over Iran. Is the prince of Persia the same as the spirit of Islam? We do not know for sure. But there are two possibilities.

The first possibility is that this dark spirit still rules over Iran. With the invasion of Islam in Iran, this spirit did not lose its position; it merely changed methods of ruling.

At the time of Daniel, the religion of Zoroastrianism was that dark spirit. After Islam took over Iran in AD 651, that same spirit chose to rule Iranian minds, hearts, and spirits via Islam.

The second possibility is that this dark spirit was defeated and displaced by the spirit of Islam. So now it is not the prince of Persia that rules Iran spiritually, but the spirit of Islam. If this is the case, then the spirit of Islam is even stronger than the prince of Persia.

In either case, a very strong dark spirit called Islam has been ruling Iran for the past 1,400 years. And this is a spirit that even the Archangel Michael struggled to deal with.

In Jeremiah 49:34-35, we read that the highest-ranking general, the Lord of Hosts will Himself destroy the dark spirit of Islam over Iran. He has already begun that task.

The good news is that this war has already started, and the destruction of Iranians' spiritual chains is under way. The dark religious spirit has been losing its grip on Iranians' hearts and souls ever since the 1979 revolution. At that time, Islam ruled the hearts of Iranians. That is why Khomeini easily took over and became Supreme Leader. He already had a foothold and control over the hearts of the masses, through their Islamic beliefs.

In Jeremiah 49:34–35, we read that the highest-ranking general, the Lord of Hosts Himself between will and destroy the dark spirit of Islam over Iran. He has already begun that task.

But now things have changed.

Millions of Iranians have rejected Islam, and that number is growing rapidly. Spiritual eyes have been opened, and they have seen that the Islamic emperor has no clothes. Islam has been discredited. Many have come to believe that Islam is *not* from God. Some have dared to say Islam is from Satan. The Islamic government held the people's hearts in the 1980s, but today they are losing control. That is why leaders have resorted to violence to control the people.

But, according to Jeremiah 49:35, the final blow will come when our Lord, the Lord of Hosts, defeats what is left of the Prince of Persia, the Spirit of Islam, and all its armies.

At the time of revolution, the people followed Islam because they loved it. Today, they follow Islam because they fear the government, not Allah.

Allah has been losing big-time in Iran. But, according to Jeremiah 49:35, the final blow will come when our Lord, the Lord of Hosts, defeats what is left of the Prince of Persia, the Spirit of Islam, and all its armies.

To summarize, the Lord will destroy all of Iran's bases of power (military, economic, political, and spiritual) to wean Iranians from Islam and humble them so that they will see their desperate need for God. This is igniting a spiritual revival that will engulf Iran and allow God to establish His throne there.

The good news: This has already begun. Despite the suffering that Iranians endure (and will continue to endure), the Lord is blessing Iran by doing something great. He is destroying the powers of darkness to set Iranians free.

Generally, a Muslim is not allowed to think critically about Islam, or question the faith or its leaders. When I was a research scientist, I witnessed to super-intelligent Muslim colleagues, prominent people with doctoral degrees. Our spiritual discussions would usually follow a pleasant path. But when we discussed Islam logically, I could sense fear and confusion invading their minds.

Praise the Lord! That spirit of fear and confusion has been lifting from Iran and Iranians.

Praise the Lord! That spirit of fear and confusion has been lifting from Iran and Iranians. Millions of Iranians are thinking logically, with an open mind. They are freely questioning their inherited religion, a faith that was forcefully imposed on them. Many Iranian Muslims are watching our satellite broadcast because they want to compare Islam with Christianity.

As a result, they are coming to Christ. For anyone with an unbiased and inquiring mind, Muhammad is no match for Jesus. The Quran is no match for the Bible, and Islamic theology is no match for the Christian faith. There is no one in the history of the world whose character and teachings are as attractive as Jesus's. He is always a winner.

WHERE HAS THE LORD ALLOWED YOU TO BE BROKEN?

In this chapter, we saw that the Lord will allow Iran to be broken to make it ready for salvation, revival, and transformation. Brokenness can make us bitter or better. Jesus has frankly told us that in this life we will face tribulation and suffering. He is not the source of injustice and suffering. Rather, He is so powerful and loving that He wants to use even the bad things for our good.

I have endured various types of suffering. Being a church planter and pastor ministering among Iranian Muslims for more than thirty years, I have faced unfair criticisms and judgments, rejections and betrayals. I have built up and given away (with gladness) many churches and ministries. However, some of these were "kidnapped" (stolen) from me. For many years, I have suffered from various physical ailments, as well as deep marital problems.

However, the most suffering and brokenness has come from the chronic sickness of Hanniel, our eldest daughter.

When a loved one suffers and you cannot do anything about it, the brokenness goes deeper and deeper into your soul. It affects your entire existence. When answers to your prayers for healing are delayed (or seem to go unanswered), you understand what is truly important in life, and what is not.

I had been a pastor for many years before Hanniel was stricken with a life-threatening sickness, but through it, my compassion for others multiplied. I recall crying and praying all night when my daughter was in emergency care, suffering from unbearable pain and battling for her life.

You must be broken before you are truly and deeply blessed. I have found that brokenness makes us humble. Then God gives grace to the humble, and lifts us up at the due time (1 Peter 5:5-6).

So now I can see, feel, and cry for the suffering of others. During our live satellite broadcast, I look into the camera and address people I can't actually see. But the Lord gives me great compassion for their suffering, and I cry. I feel their desperation because I often have endured desperate times myself.

Suffering is unpleasant, and we want to evade it at all costs. We hope we can find a shortcut to victory and the power of His resurrection, without experiencing the suffering of the cross. But I have learned this spiritual principle: You must be broken before you are truly and deeply blessed. I have found that brokenness makes us humble. Then God gives grace to the humble, and lifts us up at the due time (1 Peter 5:5-6).

Most of the blessings and victories in my life have come after a season of desperate suffering. Every great suffering has launched me to a new level of spiritual maturity, a new level of intimacy with the Lord. I suspect this will continue until He returns or I go to Him.

After every season of hardship and adversity, He has elevated our ministry to a new level of effectiveness and impact.

Go deeper in your relationship with Jesus. Fall in love with Him afresh. Let Him love you like never before.

I am sure you could share similar stories from your life. I'm sure the Lord has blessed you through suffering and added physical and spiritual blessings that you could not get any other way. If you are suffering today, please don't resist it. Don't get bitter against the world, against those who have caused your suffering, or against the Lord.

Go deeper in your relationship with Jesus. Fall in love with Him afresh. Let Him love you like never before. Let Him do His work in you, change you, and make you a better person—a more qualified child of God to do a greater work for Him.

This spiritual principle of suffering and blessing works at all levels. It applies to individuals, families, churches, cities, and even nations.

A family's suffering can make it stronger and healthier. As I have experienced, it can bring family members closer to each other and to God. It can help family members appreciate each other more, and appreciate even the smallest blessing.

When I am with my children, I cherish every minute. This mindset makes family members more compassionate. Additionally, this mindset is contagious, allowing one family to impact others.

As with a family, for a nation to be blessed, it must first be broken. Then it will be blessed so abundantly that it will become a blessing to other nations. The United States was founded by desperate and broken people who escaped their suffering in Europe, only to suffer even more in the new land. That is one reason the Lord has used this country to bless so many countries in the past 250 years.

CHAPTER 10

THERE WILL BE A HORRIBLE WAR IN IRAN

IRANIANS LOVE AMERICANS. Are you shocked? It is true. They love and admire America and everything American. They love American culture. They love American music and American movies.

If they ever get a chance, they will want a democracy in Iran—American style. Many Iranians love America and respect its flag more than some Americans do. You don't hear that in the news. I encourage you to listen to what the Lord says about Iran in Jeremiah 49:34-39 than what the news says about Iran.

God can use us where we are to love those He has already placed around us for His glory.

Now, let's continue our verse-by-verse study of Jeremiah 49:34-39.

The first question is: When do you think the Lord will break the bow of Elam? We don't know when. But we know it is going to be horrible.

JEREMIAH 49:36

"I will bring upon Elam the four winds from the four ends of heaven, and will scatter them to all these winds; and there will be no nation to which the outcasts of Elam will not go."

Here, the scattering of Iranians among the world's nations is predicted. Nowhere in recorded history have we seen the people of Iran (or Elam) be scattered worldwide.

Only after the 1979 revolution did Iranians leave their country to become immigrants (or refugees) to various nations of the world. This recent dispersion of Iranians is just the beginning of this prophecy's fulfillment. Its ultimate fulfillment is still ahead of us, when the horrible war described in Jeremiah 49:37 will occur.

"The four winds from the four ends of heaven"—This phrase "four winds" appears nine times in the Bible. The interpretation can be literal, symbolic, or both. Almost any biblical prophecy can be viewed from these angles. Usually, the best and most complete understanding of prophecies requires literal (physical) *and* symbolic (spiritual) interpretations.

As we see in the Bible, visible (earthly) events are often closely connected to invisible events in the spiritual world. The word wind, *ruach* in Hebrew, has a double meaning. It can refer to physical wind and "spirit wind."

The Lord often uses earthly forces to accomplish His goals.

By studying the phrases "four winds" and "four ends of heaven," we see that (primarily) they should be interpreted figuratively. This means that *all* of the heavenly (spiritual forces) will be involved in the scattering and dispersion to the whole world.

How will heaven's spiritual forces cause Iranians to scatter? The Lord often uses earthly forces to accomplish His goals.

For example, after years of warning the Northern Kingdom (Israel), the Lord used Assyrians to inflict punishment. And the Lord used Babylonians to fulfill His prophecy (in Jeremiah 25:9-12) that the Southern Kingdom (Judah) would be taken captive. When Jesus prophesied that the Jews would be taken to exile (Luke 21:24), the Roman Empire fulfilled that prophecy and scattered the Jews to countries under Roman rule.

The Bible repeatedly shows us that events initiated in heaven are fulfilled through earthly means. God usually fulfills His will through His children. Many are fulfilled through obedient Christians who seek to know Him and His will. But sometimes God accomplishes things through people who do not even know Him.

The dispersion of Iranians will be initiated by the spiritual forces of heaven, but will be fulfilled by earthly forces that will cause Iranians to scatter throughout the world.

The word "heaven" in this passage (*shamayim* in Hebrew) can also mean "sky." Today, we understand that future wars will be fought (primarily) from the air, with planes, drones, and (soon) flying intelligent robot soldiers. So it is consistent with modern warfare strategy that Iran will face an all-out air strike.

Our Scripture passage makes it obvious that Iran will be attacked by outside forces. Taking "four winds" literally, perhaps Iran will be attacked from all sides, by many countries.

For example, Afghanistan (east of Iran) and Iraq (to the west) could be used by the United States and/or other countries to launch an attack on Iran. Saudi Arabia and the countries of United Arab Emirates (UAE) fear Iran, so they would certainly allow their land and airspace to used for an invasion. They and their allies can use US bases in Kuwait, Bahrain, and the UAE itself for such purposes.

Even if these countries change their minds and do not cooperate, the United States Navy in the Persian Gulf has enough power to launch an extensive and effective attack on Iran.

BUT WHAT ABOUT AN ATTACK FROM THE NORTH?

If this passage in Jeremiah 49 is taken literally, then an attack from the north could happen two ways. In one scenario, Russia has already been judged. Indeed, if Ezekiel 38:16-22 has already been fulfilled, Gog (Russia) has faced the Lord's harsh judgment and either does not exist, or is so weak and subdued that other countries are using it to launch an attack on Iran.

Currently, Russia and Iran have a good relationship. The more the United States, Israel, and other countries in the West threaten Iran, the closer the relationship between Iran and Russia becomes. This strategic alliance could remain strong for years, until the prophecies of Ezekiel 38 occur. This alliance is clearly ill-fated, because Russian leaders, who do not believe God exists, are paired with Iranian leaders, who claim to be God's representatives on earth.

In the second scenario, Russia will betray the two countries' friendship by invading Iran from the north. Russia has always wanted Iran as a part of its territory, so that it can gain access to the oil and the warm waters of the Persian Gulf.

Many of the territories in southern Russia were part of Persia for many centuries, until recent times. Early in the 19th century, after a brief war between Russia and Iran, a treaty called Turkmenchay was signed. The treaty stipulated that the lands containing the current countries of Georgia, Armenia, and Azerbaijan would be handed over to Russia. Meanwhile, the Aras River (in northern Iran) was set as the new border between the two countries.

Late in the 19th century, Iran was forced to sign another contract giving the central Asian territories (which had been under Persian rule for centuries) to czarist Russia. These territories comprise modern Uzbekistan, Kazakhstan, Turkmenistan, and Tajikistan.

Then, in 1941, Russia invaded and occupied northern Iran, hoping to claim that territory. They didn't leave until well after World War II (in May of 1946), after Iran complained to the United Nations Security Council.

It's possible, then, that Russia will betray Iran to fulfill its long-term dream to "own" the country. And this invasion might not create much controversy, because the world will already be in chaos. Some nations might even welcome the invasion.

"There shall be no nation to which the outcasts of Elam will not go"—The scope of Iranians' dispersion will be so great that there will be *no nation* where Iranians will not immigrate (flee). If this prophecy appeared anywhere but the Bible, we would be skeptical, saying, "Do you really believe that all of the 194 nations recognized by the United Nations will have Iranian immigrants?"

The answer is "Yes, for the Bible says so."

By the way, it is already happening.

Like many other prophecies, the fulfillment of this prophecy has begun, setting the stage for its *ultimate* fulfillment. After all, Iranians have been scattering throughout the world since 1979, and their dispersion is not slowing down.

Currently, more than 7 percent of the world's 80 million Iranians (almost 6 million people) live outside of Iran. For example, approximately one million Iranians live in the United States. Travel the whole world, and you will find few nations that are not home to Iranians.

For example, I met a recent Iranian immigrant at the Iranian Christian Church of Sunnyvale, CA. Here is a summary of our conversation:

"Where were you before you came to the United States?"

"I was living at Tongatapu."

"Where is that?"

"It is part of the archipelago of Tonga."

"Where is Tonga?"

"It is south of Samoa."

"Were you there alone?"

"No, there were many Iranians there. Some were there temporarily, waiting for a decision on their immigration request to the United States. But there were some Iranians living there permanently."

In another conversation, I shared the Iran prophecy with an Englishman in London. He told me, "I believe it. It is already happening. Last year, I wanted to vacation at someplace new. Not too far from home, but unknown to tourists and *quiet.* A place to explore and rest. I asked my travel agent to find me such a place.

"She looked in her books for a few minutes and said 'I have a perfect place for you. It is a small island in the North Sea.' Then she mentioned a place that I hadn't heard of.

"I told her, 'That's a great choice; I will go there.' When I told people where I was going, they were astonished because they had never heard of the island. But I went, and I loved that island. It was beautiful. Not many people lived there, but I met an Iranian doctor who lived there and had set up his practice!"

Here is something unusual about Iranian immigrants. Usually, the weak, the poor, and the uneducated emigrate from a country. For Iran, it is the opposite. Most Iranian immigrants are educated, many are business people, and a good number are wealthy. I don't share the following information to boast or inflate my ego as an Iranian American. Instead, I want to build a case for how Jeremiah 49:36 can be fulfilled in the future:

According to the International Monitory Fund (IMF), Iran ranks the highest in brain drain among the ninety countries that they surveyed (which included developed and less-developed countries). According to the IMF, more than 150,000 of Iran's best young minds leave the country every year.[8]

It is estimated that one-fourth of college-educated Iranians eventually leave the country. The Dean of Stanford University has stated that Iran's Sharif University of Technology has the world's best under-graduate electrical engineering school.[9] And, at one time, Iranian students admitted to Stanford's doctoral engineering program outnumbered the university's home-grown undergrads. (And most of those Iranian students had earned scholarships.)

It is no wonder that most Iranian immigrants become successful in their host countries. Given time, they establish themselves well. As a pastor in California, I helped many immigrants move to the United States and settle there.

On several occasions, I helped people who had to start from zero. In the beginning, they were struggling so much that we had to use some of our church benevolence funds to buy them groceries.

Some had to start with dishwashing jobs. But fast-forward ten years, and these same Iranians were running their own businesses. Some lived in expensive houses in Silicon Valley and owned several cars.

Recently, one of my American friends in California decided to go on an African jungle safari. When he returned, he told me this astonishing story:

> "We were in the middle of nowhere, deep inside the jungle. We told our tour guide, 'We're thirsty and need a place we can buy a safe bottled drink.' He took us to a nearby small village. There we found a shop owned by an Iranian businessman who lived there. This man was smart. His shop was at the right place, selling what tourists needed most: Coca-Cola and American goodies! It was obvious he was doing just fine financially."

Most Iranians are doing fine wherever they go. In the United States, many Iranians have risen to the top of their field, professionally and financially. Here are just a few: Pierre Omidyar (founder of eBay), Anousheh Ansari (a successful engineer and telecommunications executive and the first female private space explorer), Omid Kordestani (executive chairman at Twitter), Sundar Pichai (CEO of Google), Arash Ferdowsi (co-founder and former CTO of Dropbox), Christiane Amanpour (CNN's chief international anchor), Jimmy Delshad (mayor of Beverly Hills), and tens of thousands more leaders in science, art, business, education, media, and government.

What does this have to do with the fulfillment of the prophecy in Jeremiah 49:39?

When the horrible war described in Jeremiah 49:35-38 happens, millions of Iranians will leave Iran and go to all nations of the world. The foundation for fulfilling that prophecy has already been laid.

How will Iranians disperse to every nation, and how will they be admitted to all these nations? After all, some nations do not accept immigrants—unless they already have close relatives there, relatives who are well-established, and are willing and able to sponsor them and assist them with the immigration process.

Currently, almost all Iranian families have a family member or a close friend who has left Iran and settled successfully somewhere in the world.

The dispersion mentioned in verse 36 must happen in a rather short time, because in Jeremiah 49:39 we see people already settled in their new land who are returning to their motherland.

It has taken over forty years for Iranians to scatter and then settle in so many nations. This explains why verses 35 and 39 can be fulfilled in such a short time frame.

JEREMIAH 49:37

"'So I will shatter Elam before their enemies and before those who seek their lives; and I will bring calamity upon them, even My fierce anger,' declares the LORD. 'And I will send out the sword after them until I have consumed them."

Here the Lord declares the ultimate judgment that will come upon Iranians. The picture is horrific. Iran's people are terrified, defeated, and shattered by their enemies. They are being killed as they flee. The scale of destruction and death is so wide that it threatens Iran's existence.

Those who left the country earlier will be in much better shape as they watch from a distance while millions of Iranians (many of their friends and family members) are being killed. Those who remained in Iran will suffer greatly, wishing they had immigrated earlier.

It is interesting that Iran's government forces Christians to emigrate from the country, in hopes of curbing Christianity's growth. When Christians are arrested in Iran, instead of going to jail, many are given their passports and told to leave the country. If not, they will face long jail sentences or execution.

"So I will shatter Elam before their enemies and before those who seek their lives"—The word "shatter" (*chathath* in Hebrew) has a primitive root, meaning "to prostrate." "Shatter" can refer to physical violence, figurative destruction through fear or confusion, or a combination of the two.

The word "before" (*paniym* in Hebrew) means "in the face of" or "in the presence of." Picture a face-to-face confrontation in which Iranians will feel horrified and utterly helpless before their enemies. After an intense air strike on strategic targets (as described in the previous chapter), the ground war will begin.

Note that there are multiple enemies involved. It appears that Iran will do something so horrible that many countries will unite to attack. Other countries will opt out of the attack, but they won't condemn it. They certainly won't come to Iran's defense.

Before speculating about this Iranian wrongdoing, let's study the verse further:

"And before those who seek their life"—These enemies will do more than defeat the Iranians. Mere victory is not enough for them. They are *determined* to take Iranian lives. The Old Testament contains several words for "life," but the only word consistently and clearly used to depict physical life is *nephesh*, which literally means "breath."

So there is no way around it. Iran's opponents are there to kill.

Again, we must ask why. What will cause Iran's enemies to launch such a bloody attack? It seems that they want revenge, a settling of accounts. They want justice, as they define it. We will explore possible scenarios later in this chapter, but, for now, let's continue our study.

"'And I will bring calamity upon them, even my fierce anger,' declares the Lord"—The word "bring" ("bow" in Hebrew) is used elsewhere in the Old Testament. It means "to bring to a location" (as in Genesis 6:19 and Exodus 23:19) or "to bring to a person or group." (See Leviticus 5:8 and Esther 1:11.)

The word "calamity" is *rah* in Hebrew. It is used to illustrate ten or more various shades of evil, depending on context. Meanings range from "slightly bad" to "utterly evil." That is the context here. We are talking about a situation that could not be any worse. People will believe that the forces of evil have been loosed on them, with no restraints. The goal is to kill and destroy.

We should expect no less. After all, we are talking about the Lord's "fierce anger." What could be worse? The Most Powerful is now The Most Angry!

When the Lord's anger is released, it always results in accomplishing His specific purposes (Jeremiah 30:24). As we learned earlier, this anger is often manifested through human oppressors (Jeremiah 25:38). These "enemies" are nations—probably non-believing, Christ-rejecting nations—that are executing God's anger and accomplishing His will for Iran.

"'And I will send out the sword after them until I have consumed them—Here we see people being killed as they are fleeing. They are being attacked from behind. We saw this in the Gulf War of 1991, when the Iraqi army was attacked and destroyed on the "Highway of Death" while retreating from the occupation of Kuwait.

What happened on that highway is consistent with the picture we get when we read "send the sword after them." The Iraqi army was dismayed, and its soldiers were fleeing. However, the air force and guided missiles were "sent after them." The attack on that highway was not intended to damage Iraq's army, but to utterly *destroy* it. The United States and its allies wanted to keep attacking until they "consumed" the Iraqi army.

You get the picture, right?

This and possibly worse will happen in the upcoming war on Iran.

WE MUST WARN PEOPLE OUT OF LOVE

This utter destruction does not mean, however, that all Iranians will be killed. The Lord intends to rule over them later, be their king, and bless them.

Joel C. Rosenberg, a best-selling prophetic writer and Middle East scholar, believes that these verses apply only to those in power in Iran. That means the Lord will destroy the religious leaders, the army, the Revolutionary Guard, and the Basij (a paramilitary organization formed by Khomeini in 1979). I agree with Joel.

When Joel appeared on our live satellite TV broadcast in September 2013 (via our studios in Dallas), he turned to the camera and frankly addressed Iran's leaders. He told them, "These are warning signs to you. If you do not repent of your sins and believe in Jesus Christ, you shall be judged and utterly destroyed."

He even called out Supreme Leader Khamenei personally, urging him to repent and believe in Jesus Christ so that he might be saved and spared from this upcoming judgment.

Joel's words were forthright and candid. They echoed the harsh judgments of Old Testament prophets. I know Joel, and I know his deep love for the Lord, which compels him to love Jews *and* Muslims. I have seen him weep as he passionately prays for the persecuted Christians and for the salvation of Iran's Muslims.

On the air, however, I realized that people who did not know Joel personally, could misunderstand what he was saying. They could (wrongly) perceive him as a Muslim-hating Jew, someone hatefully threatening Iran's leaders. I was nervous and did not want to finish the live broadcast on that tone.

I prayed in my heart and asked the Lord to give me wisdom, to give me closing remarks that left no room for misunderstanding. I didn't want to give our enemies a chance to misuse the broadcast to sow evil and animosity between Jews and Iranian Muslims.

The Lord was gracious to answer my heart prayer. He gave me wisdom on the spot for wrapping up the broadcast. By His inspiration, I finished the program by addressing viewers and Iran's leaders:

> "If you love somebody who is in danger of losing their lives, you will warn them. You do not warn them because you hate them, but because you love them. There is a judgment coming. It is written in the Bible, so it is certain that it will happen. We do not hate you if you are a political, military, or religious leader of Iran. We love you because the Lord loves you and wants to save you. Because of that love, we have to reveal the upcoming judgment. We do not want to see you killed and destroyed. Repent while there is time."

That broadcast created quite a stir. We put it on our Facebook page, and tens of thousands of people quickly downloaded it. We heard reports of people inside Iran duplicating and distributing the broadcast by the thousands. It has become one of our most downloaded videos.

Again, I believe this harsh judgment will not affect all of Iran's people. It will target the country's ruling segment.

Here is another hint to consider. The word "consume" in this verse is *kalah* in Hebrew. It means "to accomplish, to finish, and to complete." Kalah is used in Genesis 2:1-2, where the Lord "finishes" or "completes" His work of creation and rests. So even though all verses in this passage indicate harsh and severe judgment, God will not destroy Iran completely. Rather, this judgment is meant to achieve God's purposes for the nation.

HAVE YOU EVER BEEN DISCIPLINED BY THE LORD?

What we have seen in this chapter is consistent with God's character. He is a good father. As a good father, He disciplines. His discipline always has a purpose, and that purpose is the good of His children.

God divides the world's people into two groups: 1) His children—people who are saved by their faith in Jesus Christ and have joined His family. 2) Those who are not yet His children—people who are not yet saved. God wants these people to put their faith in Christ and become His children.

For His children, God uses the suffering present in the world, as well as divine discipline, to mature them, to help them become more like Jesus. This way, they can grow into receiving their full inheritance in Christ.

For those not yet Christians, He uses the sufferings of this world to help them realize their need for God and to seek Him and His salvation.

I have seen this in my own life. I love the exhortation in Hebrews 12:1-3 to set aside every sin and whatever hinders me to look at Jesus as my example and run the course He has set before me, and to be ready to suffer as He did and not be discouraged by people's hostility. Nevertheless, many times when I have been distracted by temptation and have failed to resist sin (as described in Hebrews 12:4), God has stepped in as a father and firmly disciplined me—while reminding me that He loves me and this is for my own good, according to Hebrews 12:5-11. The Lord seems to be saying, "I want you to live according to Hebrews 12:1-3, but if you don't (and act like Hebrews 12:4), then as a good father, I will act like Hebrews 12:5-11."

This principle is true for individuals and nations. We have learned that the Lord will discipline Iran. At the same time, Scripture assures us that His harsh discipline will lead to salvation and great blessings for the nation.

What about you? Is the suffering of this world pushing you towards the love of God? If you have not received God's love expressed to you through Jesus, is your experience in this unjust and cruel world convincing you that you need Him? If you have already put your faith in Jesus, have you experienced God's fatherly discipline to mature you? How is your current suffering is shaping you to become more like Jesus?

CHAPTER 11

GOD WILL SET HIS THRONE IN IRAN!

HOW DOES GOD go from being angry to being our Savior? How does He go from judging us to blessing us? As we search the Scriptures, we see that God gets angry and is moved to action by sin, disobedience, rebellion, injustice, and so on. For Iran, He first will be angry and judge it before saving and blessing it. He is wanting the reader to ask the question in the heading directly below.

HOW DO WE CONNECT EZEKIEL 38 AND JEREMIAH 49?

Here is the brief answer: According to Ezekiel 38:1-6, Magog (Russia), with its mostly Islamic allies (including Persia/Iran), will attack Israel. This is generally called "The War of Gog and Magog." In Ezekiel, the Lord states that because of this attack, His fierce anger is provoked and He will judge Russia and all the other nations that attacked Israel. That includes Iran, and we can read about this prophecy's fulfillment in Jeremiah 49:34-37.

But there is a problem: In Ezekiel 38, it is Persia that attacks Israel, but in Jeremiah 49, it is Elam that the Lord punishes. How come?

First, both Persia and Elam are a part of today's Iran.

So both prophecies are relevant here. Second, Iran (Persia) will attack Israel, according to Ezekiel 38. This attack will manifest God's fierce anger and judgment. But the retaliation will focus on the Elam province of Iran. And that, as we have learned, is the location of the oil wells, nuclear facilities, and nuclear missiles aimed at Israel.

There are many clues that connect the events of Ezekiel 38 and Jeremiah 49. The events of Jeremiah 49:34-37 will happen after, and as a result of, events in Ezekiel 38. Here are seven pointers:

1. *Similar Wrath of God*—In both passages, God's wrath is provoked, which leads to punishment. The Lord's anger is expressed in Ezekiel 38:18-19: "It will come about on that day, when Gog comes against the land of Israel,' declares the Lord God, 'that My fury will mount up in My anger. In My zeal and in My blazing wrath I declare *that* on that day there will surely be a great earthquake in the land of Israel." The Lord's anger in this passage is consistent with His "fierce anger" in Jeremiah 49:37.
2. *Similar Judgments*—Note that the judgments in these two passages are similar in their intensity. But this does not mean that they are the same. The judgments in Ezekiel 38-39 take place in Israel, but the judgment of Jeremiah 49 happens in Iran. It is the same judgment for the same reason, but administered in two different locations. As we shall see, the times of these two judgments are close to each other. So we can conclude that the events of Jeremiah 49 happen shortly after the events of Ezekiel 38-39.

3. *Iran is in Both Judgments*—The judgment proclaimed in Ezekiel 38 is for Gog, but it is also "on the many peoples who are with him (Gog)" (Ezekiel 38:22). This includes Iran. Iran is punished in Jeremiah 49 and Ezekiel 38 for being part of Gog's army that attacks Israel. As a confirmation, Ezekiel 32:24-25 describes the horrible judgment on Elam in even more detail.
4. *Similar Timing*—Both judgments and their associated events will happen in the "latter years" (Jeremiah 49:30 and Ezekiel 38:8, 16). They are not from a different era in human history. They are closely related events; one will closely follow the other.
5. *Similar Results*—Both of these events will result in the salvation of nations. In Ezekiel we read repeatedly that all this judgment and horrible events will manifest God's glory in the world. Many nations will see and know that glory. In Jeremiah, we see that these events will result in all of Iran knowing the Lord so deeply that He can state that He rules in Iran and He is their King (Jeremiah 49:38).
6. *Similar Thrones*—The Jews' salvation, mentioned in the Ezekiel passage (Ezekiel 39:21-22), is a precursor for establishing God's throne in Jerusalem (Jeremiah 3:17 and Micah 4:2). We also see that His throne will be set in Elam (Jeremiah 49:38). These two events cannot be too far apart, but which will happen first? We don't know, but the Bible says that the salvation of Gentiles makes the Jews jealous. (See Romans 11:11.) Perhaps the Lord will save Iran first. Then when the Jews shall see that their archenemies are now their friends, they will open up to the Gospel message.
7. *Similar Russian Betrayal of Iran*—Ezekiel 38:21 prophesies that the coalition of nations who attack Israel will collapse. We will see, "Every man's sword will be against his brother," killing and destroying each other. Could this be a precursor

to the fulfillment of Jeremiah 49:36-37 when Iran will be attacked from its north (e.g., from Russia)? Before that, Gog and Magog will almost be destroyed during the events of Ezekiel 38-39. So, a weakened Russia might join more powerful nations to attack Iran. But even if they do not participate in the attack on Iran, Russian land—willingly or unwillingly—could be used for that purpose.

WILL IRAN FACE A SECOND JUDGMENT?

Here is another question to consider: After severe judgment on Iranians (along with Russia), as described in Ezekiel 38-39, why would the Lord punish Iran further by attacking the country, destroying its base of power, and sending His sword there? Why wouldn't the first punishment be enough? The answer? The Iranian government will be doing something else to wound God's heart, so His fury will mount against them. (Ezekiel 38:18).

What could that "something" be?

As we study the Bible, we see that God has a special plan for Israel and the Jews, but He also cares about His Church and has a plan for it too. He is passionate about both. He calls Israel "the apple of His Eye" (Zechariah 2:8), and He considers His Church to be His Bride, His own body, and one with Him. Remember how He admonished Paul on the way to Damascus?

"Why are you persecuting Me?" (Acts 9:4).

God loves Israel, but He also loves His Church. He has a special plan for Israel, but He also has a special plan for His children. Because of His passion for Israel, His fierce anger will be ignited and activated. (See Ezekiel 38-39.)

God loves Israel, but He also loves His Church. He has a special plan for Israel, but He also has a special plan for His children.

In a similar way, His passion and love for His Church will ignite His fierce anger in the end times. The end-time judgment will occur immediately after a worldwide persecution and killing of Christians.

In fact, Iran's government has been persecuting Christians for years. This persecution is likely to increase. So, Iran will attack Israel and continue to intensify its persecution of the Lord's children inside Iran.

Can you imagine God helping Israel but not His children (the Church)? Would He judge those who attack Israel while ignoring the intense persecution of His children at the hands of the Iranian government? Yes, the Lord loves Israel, but He is also passionate about His children, including the Iranian Christians.

Again, this persecution has already started in Iran. And it intensifies year after year. The Church in Iran has been under pressure (and increasing persecution) since the Islamic Revolution of 1979.

In recent times, after a public declaration of war against Christians and underground house churches by Ali Khamenei (in November of 2011), the church has suffered an intense season of arrests, imprisonment, and torture.

Many precious men and women of God, some of whom I know personally, have been jailed and tortured. The courage and the sweet spirit of those who have been tortured, and their loving and forgiving heart toward their torturers, have touched my own life deeply and permanently. These are today's heroes of faith.

As this brutality against Christians intensifies, it will provoke the Lord's anger. So He will take another step of judgment, bringing destruction to Iran's leaders, so that His Church will flourish and grow in influence, until Iran becomes a Christian nation under the rule of Christ.

These two sets of prophecies regarding judging Iran and saving Iran *will* happen, and they will happen simultaneously: *The government of Iran* will follow through with its threat to wipe Israel off the map and will partner with Russia to do so. As a result, the Ezekiel 38 prophecies will be fulfilled. It will intensify its persecution of Christian.

On the other hand (and at the same time), *the people of Iran* will continue to turn their backs to Islam and their Islamic government. They will dedicate their lives to their new-found Savior, whom they love and obey with all their might. They will continue to grow stronger and deeper in their faith, until the prophecy in Jeremiah 49:38 is fulfilled and His throne is set in Iran.

After Iran's political leaders are judged and removed, millions of persecuted (but strong) Iranian Christians will have the freedom to function in the society. As a result, they will transform Iran. This will turn Iran into an openly Christian nation, via a natural transforming influence of Christians over Iran's government, media, finance, education, and artistic community.

In summary, the events of Jeremiah 49 (regarding Iran) and Ezekiel 38 are closely related. God's judgment on Iran in Jeremiah 49 continues the judgment began in Ezekiel 38, for similar reasons and motivations, in a similar manner, and with similar goals and results.

It is clear: Iran will join Russia and others in attacking Israel. That will bring the Lord's "fierce anger." He will judge Russia, Iran, and other nations in that coalition. But the Lord will judge Iran further because of its severe and brutal persecution of His Church. (See Jeremiah 49:35-37.)

The final results in both places will be similar: the salvation of many Jews and Iranians and the establishment of God's throne in Jerusalem and Iran. Yes, as the Bible has recorded, the histories of Iran and Israel are connected. And, as the Bible prophesies, the *futures* of Iran and Israel will be closely connected as well.

JEREMIAH 49:38

"Then I will set My throne in Elam and destroy out of it king and princes,' declares the LORD."

This is a most amazing prophecy, describing a bright future for Iran. God will set His throne there! That is a major promise, repeated nowhere else in the Bible and given to no other place, except Jerusalem. But first, He has to destroy what is there. Before establishing a new kingdom, He will destroy and remove the powers ruling Iran. That includes both political and spiritual powers.

"Then I will set My throne in Elam — This is more than saying "one million Muslims will come to Christ in Iran." A large scale salvation is part of the prophecy, but not all of it. You see, the numbers are important but are not enough. In the United States, there are millions of Christians, but the Lord cannot say, "I rule here."

This is more than saying "one million Muslims will come to Christ in Iran."

I live in Dallas, Texas, and there is a church (often a mega-church) on about every street corner. That is good! But the Lord cannot say, "My throne is established in Dallas." Yes, millions of believers gathering weekly in thousands of churches, worshiping powerfully and listening to great sermons is good. But it doesn't mean that the Lord's kingdom has been established here.

Let's work backwards. Someday, the Lord will say, "I have set My throne in Iran." What does that mean for Iran's future?

Of course, this means that most Iranians will become Christians, and that churches will be everywhere. But the numbers are not enough. There will be millions of Christians, yes, but these millions will know Him *intimately*. They will love Him as their King and obey Him in every area of their personal and public lives.

This will be the transformed Iran. This will be Iran as a Christian nation.

We will see millions of people who are not satisfied with attending a great church service and then returning to their "normal" lives. Instead, God will be the ruler in their personal lives, in their families, and at their workplaces—in every area of their lives. This will be the transformed Iran. This will be Iran as a Christian nation.

"And destroy out of it king and princes"—The Hebrew word for "destroy" is *abad*, a strong word. In the Bible, abad usually signifies God's destruction of evil. For example, in Numbers 33:52 it is used to order the children of Israel to destroy idols. The phrase "out of it" literally means "out of there." So He will destroy and remove "king and princes" from Iran.

WHO ARE THE KING AND PRINCES OF IRAN?

Note that the word "king" is singular. It refers to one person who is the center of all powers in a country. A king ruled Iran for over 2,700 years before the 1979 revolution. Many thought that the era of kings in Iran had come to an end, and the age of freedom and democracy had started. That is why they welcomed the Islamic revolution.

But people were set up for a major letdown. After more than forty years of Islamic rule, they have realized that they replaced King Mohammad Reza Shah and his Pahlavi dynasty with another, and much more powerful, line of kings called "Supreme Leaders."

A Supreme Leader in Iran has more power than any king in the world. He has the ultimate power and the final say in every aspect of personal and public life. This includes laws for personal and private conduct, even at home, and excuse me—even in the bedrooms and bathrooms. He has the final say in all the laws that the government passes. The Supreme Leader determines all domestic and foreign policies. He is the head of all branches of the government and military. He directly rules the media. There is no independent radio, TV, internet, or newspapers.

His power is greater than a king's, because he is officially the "deputy of God" on earth. His word and command carry as much authority as if God (Allah) has spoken. Disobeying the Supreme Leader is the same as disobeying God. It is punishable by death. Those who disagree with or question his decisions are arrested and charged with the crime of "Moharebeh ba Khoda" (warring against God). They receive long jail sentences and, often, orders of execution.

When the time for fulfillment of this prophecy comes, the Lord will destroy and remove the Supreme Leader. Moreover, He will destroy the position of "Supreme Leader" forever. Therefore, He will wipe Islam from Iran forever.

The Hebrew word for "princes" is *sarim.* "Sar" in Hebrew (as well as in Farsi) simply means "head." So this word has nothing to do with a "prince" as a son of a king. Its main meaning is ruler, leader, or government official.

The Lord is saying He will "destroy and throw out" whoever is Supreme Leader, as well as other top government leaders. If this happened today, judgment would come to the Supreme Leader, the members of the Guardian Council, the members of the Expediency Council, and the heads of the Revolutionary Guard.

JEREMIAH 49:39

"'But it will come about in the last days that I will restore the fortunes of Elam,' declares the LORD."

Here is a great hint about the timing of all these events. In verse 36 we saw that the Lord will scatter Iranians to all nations of the world. But this verse promises that He will gather them back to Iran. That will happen in the "last days," the end times before Jesus establishes His kingdom on earth.

There cannot be a great time gap between these two events. History has shown us that when the people of one nation immigrate (voluntarily or involuntarily), after two generations they consider themselves citizens of the new nation. They have no desire to go back.

Even the Jews, with their deep commitment to their land, their temple, and their God, for the most part, declined to return when Cyrus allowed them to return to their land. Specifically, only 49,942 (out of 1 million) went back. Such a low number! The majority remained in the Persian Empire. Even though Cyrus *paid them* to go back, most of them had already settled in Iran. They had families and jobs. They did not want to uproot and start all over again. They had freedom of religion where they lived. They had adapted to their host cultures. Their children were born and raised in Iran, so the Jews considered it their homeland.

In recent times, we have seen the unique return of the Jews to the motherland of Israel after World War II. This return had several unusual elements. The Jews kept their identity through centuries by living as a Jewish community wherever they lived.

Also, the Holocaust motivated many of them to seek their own land and country. That's why most of the immigrants to the new Israel were from war-stricken European countries. Relatively few American Jews made that decision, as they had comfortably settled in the United States and were doing quite well. They didn't want to start over with their lives.

Studying the behaviors of over 6 million Iranians who have left Iran in the past forty years to settle in another country, we don't see Iranians forming a strong community in foreign lands—trying to preserve their culture, language, and identity. On the contrary, Iranians tend to adjust and be absorbed in their host culture.

In the past thirty years, I have planted several churches for Iranian Muslim immigrants in the United States. I have helped many refugees settle in the United States. Many came with nothing, but they worked hard and now are doing quite well. They have businesses, cars, and homes. They love Iran, but they don't want to forsake the US lifestyle and return to Iran, even if it opens up politically.

Many Iranians who have settled in the West try to forget, deny, or downplay their heritage. They want to be considered American. Many have forgotten about Iran. They have given up on Iran. They are tired of the bad news they hear. Most have lost hope to see Iran transformed.

Many Iranians have married Americans and have kids that are more American than Iranian. They don't want to go back, unless something major compels them to do so.

I have lived in the United States since 1979. Because of my ministry and the broadcast, I am considered a public enemy by the Iranian government. I cannot go back. Because of His calling, I have a burning desire for the salvation of Muslims and especially Iranians. Meanwhile, my three children were born in the United States. They grew up in an Iranian church, were around Iranians all their lives, and have observed me, my passion, and my ministry since their childhood.

Because of His calling, I have a burning desire for the salvation of Muslims and especially Iranians.

So they have a sweet feeling for Iran. They want to see Iran saved. But the United States is their homeland. They won't return to Iran unless they are clearly called by God.

History has shown us that after two generations, immigrant families are integrated into their host culture. Their grandchildren do not even speak their original language. My children's first language is English, just as it is for all other Iranian immigrant families. Farsi is their second language.

Some families force their kids to speak Farsi at home, but most second-generation Iranian Americans don't speak Farsi very well, if at all.

And when we get to the third generation of immigrants, English is the only language they speak and understand. They speak no Farsi. They have little knowledge of Iran and its culture. Many have no special feelings for Iran. They don't want to leave the United States, which, to them, is "my country." Indeed, Iran is a "foreign land" that meant something special to their grandparents, but it was more than fifty years ago.

By matching these facts with our Jeremiah 49:39 prophecy, we can conclude the following:

There cannot be a large time gap between the dispersion of Iranians in Jeremiah 49:36 and their return in Jeremiah 49:39. The gap will probably be less than one generation (forty years), because those who return in verse 39 are the same ones who left in verse 36. These events will all happen in the "last days," close to the events of Ezekiel 38.

They will want to return because Jesus is ruling Iran. Iran will be such a transformed society that Iranians in the diaspora, as well as other Iranians, will be eager to live in a land with only two laws: Love the Lord, and love one another.

Iran will be such a transformed society that Iranians in the diaspora, as well as other Iranians, will be eager to live in a land with only two laws: Love the Lord, and love one another.

Iranians will return because they will be proud of what Iran has become. (Today, conversely, they are embarrassed to call themselves Iranians.)

They will return when they see that a better life awaits them in Iran, even better than the "good life" they have built in America. In short, verse 39 will be fulfilled (their return), because verse 38 *is* fulfilled (His throne established in Iran).

"Then I will restore the fortunes of Elam"—Let's make sure we understand what this verse is saying, because there are several ways it can be translated.

However, two variations are most widely accepted. We find the first approach in the New International Version (NIV), New American Standard Bible (NASB), English Standard Version (ESV), Good News Translation (GNT), and the Revised Standard Version (RSV). All of these Bibles use the wording "restore the fortunes of Elam."

The second group includes the King James Version (KJV) and the New King James Version (NKJV). They translate the verse, "bring about the captivity of Elam." This means that the Iranians who have been dispersed, as described in verse 36, will eventually return to their land.

I believe it is both and they are not separable.

Let's look at the text more carefully. The word "restore" in Hebrew is *shoob*, which can mean "cause to return," "make to return," or "restore." The Hebrew word for "fortunes" is *shebooth*, which *literally* means "captives," and "exiles." But *figuratively* it could mean "fortunes," and "prosperity."

I would never dare to challenge any of the above translations. Each was completed by a group of scholars who worked hard for years to accomplish a monumental task. However, it is reasonable to expect consistency in translation. A phrase must be translated consistently throughout the Bible. I understand that a word can mean different things in different contexts. However, I am not talking about one word here, but a set of words that form a phrase.

This exact phrase from Jeremiah 49:39 also appears in Jeremiah 33:7 and Amos 9:14. Almost all Bible scholars agree that these two passages foretell the return of the Jews (both Judah and Israel) to their land. (This has been fulfilled in recent years, after the end of World War II in 1945.)

So if we believe this phrase indicates the Jews' return to their land (in Jeremiah 33:7 and Amos 9:14), then the same phrase in Jeremiah 49:39 must indicate the Iranians' return to their land.

Of course, it is not hard to believe that the return of the captives could indicate the start of a new season of restoring blessing and prosperity. The Lord returns the exiles in order to give them back the wealth, success, and the glory they once had—and more. Spiritual blessing and prosperity are included, and the Lord's rule will certainly open the doors for *all kinds* of blessings.

WHAT IS GOD'S PLAN FOR YOUR LIFE?

The Lord loves all people in the world. He wants all to come to know Him and receive His salvation so that "whoever believes in Him shall not perish" (John 3:16; 1 Timothy 2:4; 2 Peter 3:9).

However, His plan for specific individuals, people groups, and nations can differ. In the Bible, He has revealed His plans for various nations, but He has something special in store for Israel and Iran: He will establish His throne in both places.

Israel shall be saved because the Bible says so. Also, Iran shall become a Christian nation and nothing can stop it, because the Bible tells us so. The fulfillment of this prophecy has already begun, as we will see in the following chapters.

How about you? God loves you and has a special plan for your life. He wants to bless you. In Jeremiah 29:11, He tells you, "For I know the plans I have for you," declares the LORD, "plans to prosper you and not to harm you, plans to give you hope and a future."

Do you know His plans for your life? Are you unsure if you have experienced God's love and salvation? Are you reading this book but aren't sure why? Are you seeking meaning in life? Whatever the case, I assure you that God is seeking you more than you are seeking Him. He is ready to transform your life. Are you ready? He wants to give you a new life and a meaningful reason to live. He has a special plan for your life.

Take the first step of surrendering your life to Him. Let Him set His throne in your heart and in your life. Let Him rule. Worship Him and obey Him. He will set you free and prosper you spiritually and in all areas of your life. He will reveal why He created you. He will use you to touch lives. Again, He is ready if you are. Just ask Him. Ask Him right now.

In your own words, make a simple request from your heart, such as, "Jesus I surrender my life to you. I am Yours, and You are mine. Wipe out my past and give me a new future."

He will do it if you ask; I assure you. If you prayed a prayer like this, please contact me and let me know, because I have been praying for you while writing these words.

PART III

IRAN IS JUST THE BEGINNING

CHAPTER 12

IRAN HAS THE FASTEST GROWING CHRISTIAN POPULATION

DID YOU KNOW that Iran has the fastest-growing evangelical population in the world[10] despite having no church buildings? And this population is led mostly by women.[11] In the film *Sheep Among Wolves Volume II*, Dalton Thomas and Joel Richardson document how the Iranian regime is losing control of this church growth and the revival among its people.

In Part II of this book, we saw that the Lord promises to set His throne in Elam (Iran). This will not happen suddenly, but over a period of time.

IRAN: A FORTY-YEAR SPIRITUAL JOURNEY

Over the past forty years, I have witnessed how Iranian Muslims have gradually walked away from Islam and the religious leaders who represent God and Islam to them. Here is what I have observed about Iranians' spiritual journey over the past 40 years:

1. Pre 1979. Before the Islamic revolution (and during the Shah's 38 years of rule), following Islam was a personal choice. Most Iranians lived a secular life outwardly, but had faith in Islam inwardly. They were neither spiritually open nor hungry to consider Christianity. The number of Muslim-background believers was in the hundreds. Christian missionaries worked hard to evangelize Muslims, with little success. Those working for the Bible Society in Iran told me, "When we were distributing Bibles, only one or two people out of one hundred would accept one—reluctantly."
2. 1980s. In the first years after the revolution, Iranians were excited that they were the only country in the world ruled by Islamic laws and led by clergy. They were sure that Islam would soon take over the world. They were ready to die for Islam. Many did die in the eight years of war with Iraq. Only a few intellectuals like me, who dared to think objectively and question Islam, came to Christ early in that decade. Eventually, hundreds of Muslims became Christians, and by the end of the decade, there were several thousand Muslim-background Christians.
3. 1990s. Iranians saw that Islamic government did not bring the promised utopia that they were dreaming about. From the beginning, the government killed its opponents. The people remembered that during the Shah's rule, they had all kinds of freedoms, except political freedom. However, they realized they had not gained political freedom—and had lost their other freedoms as well. They felt disillusioned, but still thought, *Nothing is wrong with Islam. The problem is that our Islamic government did not implement Islam correctly.*

   They started questioning the government but not Islam. However, a growing number of university students and intellectuals *did* start questioning Islam and looking at it open-mindedly. During those years, we saw a surge in the number of Muslims coming to Christ. Thousands came to Christ, as the number of Muslim-background Christians grew to tens of thousands. In 1999, there were public protests (the first since 1979), but only among students. The government responded brutally, attacking dorms and killing students in their bedrooms. Some students were killed when they were thrown out of their windows.

4. 2000s. A growing number of Iranians—not just intellectuals—started questioning Islam. After observing Islam critically, they concluded, "The problem is not that the government failed to implement Islam correctly; there is something fundamentally wrong with Islam itself." Books criticizing Islam, written decades previously, became underground best-sellers, even though they were banned by the government. In 2009, people from the middle class joined students and intellectuals in the streets, protesting during the "green movement." Tehran was the focal point of the protests; most other Iranian cities did not participate.

   Hundreds were killed. Thousands more were arrested. Many were tortured, raped, and killed while in custody. Several Christian satellite channels were launched during this decade, and they played an important role in helping people compare Christ and Christianity with Islam. We had the honor of broadcasting the first Christian program into Iran on December 1, 2001. During this decade, tens of thousands of Iranians became Christians, bringing the total to several hundred thousand.

5. 2010s. The spirit of Islam, which is the spirit of violence, fear, and deception, started losing its grip on the souls of Iranians. It was as if a veil was lifted from the minds of Iranian Muslims. In private conversations and on the internet, they dared to discuss politics, Islam's flaws, and

the life of Muhammad. Criticizing Islam became a trend, a sign of progressive thinking. The opinions formerly held only by intellectuals now spread to the middle class. Eyes were opened to see the deception, corruption, and injustices perpetrated by the Iranian government and by Islam itself. In 2018 (in response to economic pressures), people in hundreds of cities took their protests to the streets. The crowds included low-income citizens who, for decades, had supported the Islamic government. In 2019, when oil prices tripled overnight, the protests intensified. Once again, the government used violence to control the situation. More than 1,500 people were killed in the streets, and more than 12,000 were arrested. This was a wake-up call to all Iranians, even the most devout Muslims: Don't blindly follow the government or Islam. During this decade, hundreds of thousands of Iranian Muslims came to Christ, bringing the total into the millions. (Estimates ranged from 1 million to 5 million.)

6. 2020s. The disconnect between the people and the government representing Islam is growing wide and deep. Currently, most people use "we" to refer to the general population and "they" to refer those in power. Now, even the common, low-income religious people see that those in power have no heart for people. When the people protest their financial misery, the government responds by killing and arresting them.

   This and other events in early 2020 (such as shooting down a passenger plane and coldheartedly lying about it, and mishandling the COVID-19 virus) has disgusted masses of Iranians. They aren't merely criticizing and rejecting Islam; they are determined to eradicate it.

   Evidence indicates that the 2020s should see millions more Iranians come to Christ. We at Iran Alive are seeing a surge

> in the number of Iranians who are coming to Christ. Many of them confess that only six months previously, they were committed Muslims who supported the government.

Iran's Islamic Government has lost the heart of the people. Iran is ripe for transformation, and it shall be transformed if we act wisely and strategically—if we partner with God to make Iran the first Islamic nation that turns to Christ. If we work together, we could see tens of millions of Iranians turn to Christ before the end of 2020's.

Iran is ripe for transformation

Earlier in this book, I warned readers not to believe everything the media—especially Iran's government-controlled media—tells you about Iran. Do not believe the videos of the government-orchestrated rallies. Instead, believe God and His promise in Jeremiah 49:38 to save Iran.

THE CURRENT STATE OF THE CHURCH IN IRAN

After a spiritual journey that spanned four decades, Iran is experiencing a great spiritual awakening.

We need to realize that most church buildings are closed in Iran. The few churches that are open serve the Armenian and Assyrian minorities, who are forced to conduct their services in their own language, a language that Iranian Muslims do not understand.

Further, these churches are forbidden to admit any Muslim-background believers or to reach out to them in any way. The underground house churches are few, and dangerous to be a part of. It is estimated that only 5 percent of Iran's Christians attend a house church. Those who attend risk imprisonment, torture, persecution, and even death.

As noted earlier, the internet and phones are controlled and monitored by the government. To learn about God or spiritual things beyond Islam, Iranians—Muslims and Christians—must rely on satellite TV (like our channel). It is illegal to own a satellite dish and receiver in Iran, but everyone has them.

When Donnell and I first prayed, "Lord, use us to save Iran," I had no idea how this would happen. We weren't aware of the technology that would enable us to go over the heads of the mullahs (Islamic clergymen) and into people's living rooms. Technology allowed us to look Iranians in the eye and tell them about a God who, unlike Allah, is loving and gentle. He wants to have a personal relationship with each Iranian—and they can experience Him immediately.

Every week, Iranians watch Iran Alive Ministries via satellite TV. They contact us via phone, email, and social media with prayer requests and questions like, "How can I become a Christian?" They know they're putting themselves at risk by contacting us, but their spiritual hunger overcomes their fear.

They are tired of being fed lies. They are desperate for truth, love, joy, peace, salvation, and the new life that only Jesus offers. They know that we don't offer empty promises and nice Christian slogans. They see Jesus's transforming power in the lives of their friends and relatives who have become Christians.

I saw this pattern in the churches I pastored in California. When, as a church, we faced chaos, conflict, in-fighting, and division, a revival broke out. Have you ever hit rock-bottom and become disgusted with your situation, or even with yourself? If so, perhaps you, too, discovered that change doesn't happen until we reach the point of "I'm sick and tired of myself. I need to change." That takes us from "I wish to change" to "I want to change," and then to "I *must* change."

Iran has languished at rock-bottom for a long time. It is desperate for change. Iranians are crying out, "We must change."

I see this happening on a large scale. Iranians are sick and tired of the government, and of themselves.

They are disgusted that there is no love and trust in the society. Even family members deceive, betray, and defraud each other. But God is using turmoil to bring a great spiritual awakening. He is turning people's hearts toward Him. Jesus is capturing their hearts. Jesus is becoming the King of Iranian hearts. Before He rules the nation, He must rule in the heart of each individual. And when God rules a person's heart, it's evident in his or her lifestyle.

FROM IRANIAN REVOLUTION TO REVIVAL

Today, a perfect storm brews in Iran. Iran is run by Islamic clergy. It is the only country in the world that has been enforcing Islam for over forty years in all areas of society: the laws, media, education, and the arts. However, much to the clergy's dismay, Iran's post-revolution generation has rejected Islam, despite all the efforts to brainwash and control them.

A revival is sweeping Iran. When you picture revival, do you see large evangelistic meetings in stadiums? Or a large number of Christians recommitting their lives to Christ and filling up churches?

A revival is sweeping Iran.

Yes, this is the picture of revival in the West's free countries. But in a closed country like Iran, where Christian gatherings are illegal (in churches and private homes), revival looks different.

Nonetheless, I proclaim, "The revival in Iran has already started. God's Kingdom is progressively and rapidly being established in the hearts of Iranians."

From a human perspective, a gloomy storm has plagued Iran since the 1979 revolution. That storm has been destroying the good in Iran, and in many ways things are getting worse. However, from a spiritual viewpoint, there is no storm. It is not even cloudy. Heaven is open, and the Son is shining brightly.

It is said that desperation is the seedbed of revival.

It is said that desperation is the seedbed of revival. The Lord has allowed this perfect storm to linger over Iran so that the people will become so hopeless that they will call upon Him and He will save them (Psalm 50:15). Today Iranians *are* desperate. They *are* crying out, and He *is* saving them.

Yes, for more than forty years, the Islamic government has exercised total control of Iran's people, dictating every aspect of their lives according to Islamic laws. This is why people are crying out to God for salvation and are desperate for a revival. They are tired of being controlled, lied to, manipulated, abused, and treated like slaves.

The way the Iranian government treats its people is similar to how Pharaoh treated the captive Israelites in Egypt. Iranians are crying out to God for salvation, just as the Israelites did. And what God is doing now is similar to what He did then. He sent Moses to save the Israelites long ago. Today, He is sending His own Son to save the Iranians.

Iranians' desperation is so wide and deep that it engulfs every area of personal and social life. The people are ready for personal transformation, and they are desperate for social, political, and economic transformation as well.

The First Great Awakening happened in the mid-1700s in Great Britain when Jonathan Edwards, a minister and Yale graduate, refused to convert his church to the Church of England.[12] He wanted the freedom to build new churches and schools that were not subject to government control.

The Unites States was founded mainly by Christians who fled the persecution, rule, and control of government-led churches in Europe. As a result, they separated church and state, and created the best democracy in the history of the world. Experiencing the evil of religious dictatorship always opens people to new and dramatically different ideas.

In Jeremiah 49:38, we see that God promises to make Iran a Christian nation. Let's look at what "Christian nation" means. This will help us see Iran's future, and how quickly its people are moving into that future.

WHAT IS A CHRISTIAN NATION?

"There is no such a thing as a Christian nation!" a rather disturbed and angry conference participant told me last year. He stared at me intensely, as if he wanted me to back down from my statement about Iran becoming a Christian nation. I sensed that he was also testing me to see how strongly I believed in my assertion. (Was it, perhaps, just an eye-catching, ear-tingling, attention-getting empty motto fabricated for public presentations?)

I hear this statement from well-meaning brothers and sisters in Christ when they hear me boldly declare: "Iran will be a Christian nation."

Often, I know what they are thinking before they speak: *This can never happen, and I hope it never does.*

But I am not offended.

I understand them. For them, a "Christian nation" looks different from what I envision. They are looking to the past and remembering the horrible era when the Church was in power, but I am looking forward to what the Bible promises will happen in the future. When I hear what they mean by "Christian nation," I agree with them. I respond, "No way. I don't want to live in that kind of Christian nation.

Nobody wants that! Such a nation would disgrace the name of Christ. I hope we will never see such a thing on earth."

So, before we explore what a Christian nation is, let's make sure we understand what it is *not.*

WHAT IS NOT A CHRISTIAN NATION?

From a historical perspective, we don't have a clear picture of a Christian nation.

But I say we must not look back, because there has never been a Christian nation. Instead, let's look forward, because this is an end-time future event.

First, let's remember how the Roman Empire transformed from the number-one persecutor of Christians into a Christian nation. This transformation weakened Christianity rather than strengthen it. It caused Christianity to become an official state religion. All Roman citizens were automatically considered "Christians," and the clergy was supported by the state. This led to a strong organization called the "Church," but it produced a weak Christianity. We don't want that to happen again.

Then, in the Middle Ages, the Church essentially ruled Europe. History books are filled with tales of control, corruption, and the ungodly character of certain popes. There was brutality, the selling of indulgences, and the dirty politics of religious leaders. To this, we say "No, thank you! We don't want *that* again!"

Christianity reached its weakest point in history during the Middle Ages. It has taken centuries to bring back biblical Christianity—the kind that early Christians experienced in the first century—and we are not done yet.

Today, many people consider the United States a Christian nation. However, according to its constitution, the United States has never been a Christian nation, even though it was founded, largely, on Christian principles. And the country has been blessed by this.

Those who enjoy America's freedom (including some atheists, secularists, and humanists who seem to want to eradicate Christianity) benefit from the Christian principles this nation was built upon. America was founded on the principle of freedom of choice, which is a Christian value.

Even in the Garden of Eden, God gave humanity the freedom to choose. And Jesus never forced nor threatened anybody. He always offered an invitation and the freedom to accept or reject it. True faith must spring from the hearts of people; it's not mandated from above. This is another Christian virtue.

Muslims in today's United States enjoy the freedom to follow their faith and build mosques, which they shrewdly call "Islamic Cultural Centers." They do not realize that this freedom comes from a constitution that is based on Christian values, even though words like God and Christianity don't appear in the document.

Even atheists and others who are actively anti-Christians do not realize that the freedom to oppose Christianity was given to them by Christians. We all enjoy our freedom because Christians crafted a constitution that does not force Christian faith on anyone. Instead, it gives people freedom to choose. Providing freedom of religion is a Christian concept.

If Christianity is true and it transforms lives, then you do not need to force it, just show it. The light does not need government support to pierce the darkness.

A nation is not Christian because it legislates Christianity. A true Christian nation gives freedom of choice to its citizens. If Christianity is true and it transforms lives, then you do not need to force it, just show it. The light does not need government support to pierce the darkness.

Jesus is the light. "The Light shines in the darkness, and the darkness did not comprehend it" (John 1:5). Unfortunately, the Islamic world today considers the United States to be a Christian nation, a nation of light. That is not a correct observation. There are many great and dedicated Christian in America, but Christ does not rule this nation. So even though the United States is a great country, founded on some Christian principles, it's never been a Christian nation.

On our satellite TV broadcast, when I proclaim that Iran will become a Christian nation, most people (including the government officials) don't understand what I mean. They think that a Christian nation is something like today's Iran. But instead of being ruled by mullahs, it will be ruled by pastors. Instead of Islamic laws being forced upon them, it will be Christian laws. Instead of an Islamic dictatorship, it will be a Christian dictatorship. Some even think I secretly dream of becoming a Christian version of Iran's Ayatollah Khomeini!

So, *no.* Iran's becoming a Christian nation doesn't mean it will become the United States, or a Christian version of Iran's Islamic government.

WHAT WILL IRAN AS A CHRISTIAN NATION LOOK LIKE?

Please remember that the notion of Iran's becoming a Christian nation is not mine. It comes directly from Jeremiah 49:38, where the Lord says, "I will set My Throne in Elam (Iran)."

So, here is what I believe Iran will look like in the near future:

I see a nation ruled by the Lord Jesus. A throne is for a king, a ruler. But what does that mean? Jesus is not another dictator who declares, "Obey me or else." He is not another tyrant who doesn't care about your heart, someone demanding conformity to His commandments. No! Jesus cares about your heart first and foremost. He says, "My Kingdom is not of this realm" (John 18:36).

The first thing He does when you believe in Him is to give you a new heart. He rules over the hearts that are transformed by Him.

The hearts that respond to His extreme and overflowing love by joyfully loving Him back and willingly obeying Him (John 14:21).

He first rules hearts, and that authority springs from an intimate heart-to-heart love relationship with Him.

It is a nation where not all are Christians. The decision to believe and follow God has always been a matter of free choice. When God created humanity, He gave us free will. From the moment of creation, humanity could choose to believe God or not. During His millennial rule, we'll see the same thing. Some, not all, will choose to believe, even when Jesus is ruling the earth!

However, for Jesus to be the King of Iran, there must be a significant number of people who will follow Him. But His Kingdom is more than numbers.

The majority of people in a nation can be labeled Christians, but that doesn't necessarily make the nation *Christian.* In my city, Dallas, you can find a church on most street corners. However, the Lord cannot say, "I rule in Dallas."

It is a nation ruled by love. It is not the quantity of Christians that matters. It's more about the quality of their commitment. Jesus condenses all the laws into two commandments:

> You shall love the Lord your God with all your heart, and with all your soul, and with all your strength, and with all your mind; and your neighbor as yourself" (Luke 10:27).

Iran will be ruled by these two laws. Of course, commanding people to love is not enough. You can have the best commandments, but if people cannot keep them—even if they want to—then those commandments look good, but that's all they do.

To be able to obey these love commandments, we need to have a new heart and new power. Jesus does more than give us commandments. He gives us a new heart so that we *want to* obey. And He gives us the Holy Spirit so that we will *be able to* obey

His commandments. (See Ezekiel 36:26.) His grace saves us and enables us to love, and to live an exemplary life.

You will see an exuberant love for God expressed in worship and in total obedience to His Word and His Spirit. Jesus declared, "If anyone loves Me, He will keep My word; and My Father will love him, and We will come to him and make Our abode with him" (John 14:23).

There are 613 laws in the Bible, and Jesus boiled them down to two. Iran will be a country with a very brief constitution and code of law. It might contain only two items.

You can pass laws to control people's behavior, but not to change their hearts. The US Code of Federal Regulations (CFR) comprises more than 200 volumes, which describe our country's laws. Each year, more than 40,000 new laws go into effect. But there is no US law that can make us love one another.

A country transformed by the power of the Gospel, ruled by love, with Jesus as its loving King, does not need a complicated code of law.

A country transformed by the power of the Gospel, ruled by love, with Jesus as its loving King, does not need a complicated code of law. The jails will be empty, and most law enforcement personnel and judges will need to find a new line of work. Following the law of love in the home will resolve the rampant divorce problem, those bitter divorce court battles that affect Christians and non-Christians.

We do not just become better people; we become a new person. By transforming individual lives, Jesus will change the whole society of Iran.

It is a nation transformed by the Gospel. When Jesus rules, things do more than get better; they get transformed. When we put our faith in Jesus and make Him the Lord of our lives, we are transformed. We do not just become better people; we become a new person. By transforming individual lives, Jesus will change the whole society of Iran.

ARE YOU DESPERATE FOR TRANSFORMATION?

Proverbs 26:20 says, "For lack of wood the fire goes out, and where there is no whisperer, contention quiets down." Some areas of your life might be soaked from the storms of life. Wood must become dry before the fire can consume it. Iran is ready for Christ because it has hit the bottom.

It seems that the whole human race has to hit bottom before we start looking up. We must be broken before we are ready for transformation in our lives. Some of us have to suffer at our enemies' hands before we cry out for God's salvation.

Are you ready for change in your life? Are you crying out to Him to save you, to give you a new heart, and put you on the path toward a new future? Jesus is the King, but are you ready to make Him the King of your heart so that He can rule your life?

CHAPTER 13

BACK TO THE FUTURE OF IRAN

WHEN GOD SAYS, "I will set My Throne in Elam (Iran), what do you envision for Iran's future? Many people saved? Definitely! Large crowds gathering in numerous megachurches? Stadiums hosting great services? Certainly! But is that all? A transformed society is much more than that.

God will rule every segment of society, but He always starts with individuals. He loves us and died for each one of us individually. Salvation is the start of a new life, for individuals and for society.

God will rule every segment of society, but He always starts with individuals.

When you believe in Jesus, you are born again. You receive a new identity: You become God's child (John 1:12). And you live like a child of God. As Jesus did, you live to glorify the Father.

This means that you allow His heart, mind, and will to be lived out through you. God wants to transform you and make you an

God wants to transform you and make you an agent of transformation in your sphere of influence.

agent of transformation in your sphere of influence. God has strategically placed you (and each of His children) to be His agent of transformation in one of seven areas of society: Family, Church, Marketplace, Media, Arts and Sports, Education, and Government.

These seven areas are sometimes called the "seven mountains" or "seven gates" of society. In every nation (especially the United States), there is a fierce battle for the control of these seven mountains. No nation will be totally transformed by the Gospel unless all seven areas are under the Lordship of Jesus and His will is obeyed in each area.

IRAN WILL NOT BECOME A CHRISTIAN NATION OVERNIGHT

Transforming these seven areas will be a process. That process has already started, but it will reach its fulfillment when Jesus sets His throne in Iran.

To get there with the right strategy, we should ask ourselves one question: What will Iran look like when Jesus has set His Throne there?

The answer to this question can be found in the Bible. We must not look at our present or past experiences; we must envision the future.

And we should follow the Bible, not allowing past victories or defeats to influence us.

Once we have a clear view of what the end will look like, including Iran's becoming a Christian nation, the Holy Spirit, our vision-giver and strategist, will show us how to get there.

Let's look at how transformation will happen in each of these seven areas—and what they will look like under the kingship of Jesus.

THE SEVEN AREAS OF TRANSFORMATION

1. *Family Transformation:* Families are the building blocks of society. Nothing solid can be built in a society until these building blocks are strong.

God knows this, and the forces of darkness know this. After the battle for the souls of humanity, the battle for family is next on the agenda for both forces.

Any attempt to change a society that bypasses or ignores the family is doomed to fail. The story of humankind in the Bible starts with a family in Genesis and ends with a family in Revelation.

The story of the whole Bible is the destruction of God's family, then rebuilding it through Jesus Christ. A promise to be fulfilled before the "Day of The Lord" comes is the healing of family relationships:

> He will restore the hearts of the fathers to their children and the hearts of the children to their fathers, so that I will not come and smite the land with a curse (Malachi 4:6).

God loves and cares for families. He invented them, and when He is on the throne in a society, His rule will be well-reflected in healthy families.

God loves and cares for families. He invented them, and when He is on the throne in a society, His rule will be well-reflected in healthy families. His Kingdom starts with Jesus being on the throne in the hearts of individuals. Immediately after that, He will be on the throne of each family unit.

Many transformation plans have failed, and many revivals have died, because they started with individual revivals but then made the big mistake of ignoring families. They went straight to reviving and transforming the society. Where Jesus rules, He will not do that.

With Jesus on the throne in our families, our marriages do more than improve; they are transformed into something totally new.

That type of family produces godly children who love God and will serve Him all their lives. Through them, the Kingdom expands and revival continues.

The reason the seven revivals in the book of Judges lasted only one generation was that they failed to pass revival on to their children.

Under Islamic rule, Iran's family unit has disintegrated to the point of total destruction. One-third of all marriages end in divorce. Iran has one of the world's highest drug addiction rates per capita. According to Iran's government, the addiction rate is 4 percent. Other sources place the number at 10 percent.

In many families, the father, mother, and even the kids are addicted to drugs. Families have become a source of pain rather than joy. Lives are destroyed rather than built up. People's souls are being wounded, not healed.

Iranian families are in pain and total despair as they watch things get worse and worse. The good news is that they are fed up with this. They are ready for transformation!

This is why Iranian families are embracing Jesus as a family, not just individually. Once a family member experiences Jesus's healing, a light shines in the darkness, attracting other family members to Him.

When Jesus is on His throne in Iran, families will be transformed—and they will become agents of further transformation.

Again, this is already happening. One person gets saved, and that salvation goes viral, touching other relatives and friends.

Jesus's effects on families will naturally spread to other areas, including the workplace, business relationships, education, and even the government. Picture millions of healthy and vibrant families, transforming every area of the society, producing a healthy and vibrant nation. That is Iran's future according to the Bible.

2. *Church Transformation:* After family, the church is (or should be) the foundation of societal transformation. A healthy church *must* affect society.

The church is Christ's body; that's more than a metaphor. It is more literal than many of us might think. What He does in the physical realm is primarily through His body. He functions through His body.

When Jesus wants something done, He inspires, leads, and empowers His body to do it. When He rules earth during the millennium, He will rule through His body.

Unfortunately, in the West, we have accepted a limited definition of the Church. We have accepted our marginal and restricted role in the society. That has become the norm for us, and it doesn't bother us as it should. We Christians have been told, "You can't do that!" so often that we have accepted it.

People have told the Church, "You can't get involved in politics or we will take away your tax exemptions. Don't touch the schools. You have no right to witness at your workplace, even if Jesus commands you. You are not welcome in media either."

For the most part, the Church has accepted this as a norm. Some people say, "You are not allowed to be salt and light to the nation; just get into your buildings and be salt and light there, provided you do not preach against certain sins that we specify."

Of course, there are exceptions. Some churches and Christians in the West don't accept these limitations and are fighting against them. But for the most part, society is impacting the church more than the church is impacting society.

Over the years, I have helped several persecuted (and tortured) underground church believers in Iran immigrate to the United States.

You see, for a persecuted Iranian Christian, the United States is the ultimate place to be, the place that provides the freedom to practice your faith. There are many great churches staffed by wonderful pastors and teachers.

You can sing and worship to your heart's desire, as loudly as you want—without experiencing distress or persecution. You can gather in your home for a Bible study without the fear of an armed police squad storming in to arrest you and everyone else. You won't be taken somewhere for interrogation and torture until you "confess" you are a spy for a foreign country. That coerced confession won't be used to convict and sentence you without a trial. You won't face a long prison sentence or execution for your beliefs.

Given America's religious freedom, one might expect Iranian Christian immigrants to be happy here, so happy that they would never want to return to their countries. Wrong! Many of them, after spending a few months here, start missing Iran!

Make no mistake; they do *not* miss the persecution and living in fear. But they miss the deep personal and continuous experience that they had with the Lord in the midst of persecution and oppression. They tell me, "There are very kind Christians here. They are sweet and loving, but the zeal and commitment is missing in most of them."

I remember asking a twenty-something immigrant, "What is wrong? Why aren't you happy?"

She had been in the United States for a few months and was serving the Lord with me by answering phone calls from our TV viewers in Iran.

"I am thankful that I am here," she explained. "Life is easier here. There are good Christians around me, and the church is good. But there is something different here."

"What is different between here and Iran?" I asked. (Because she had lived as a Christian in both countries, she was well-qualified to answer that question.)

She explained, "It looks like there is a spirit of lethargy and drowsiness among American Christians. It is as if Satan himself is singing lullabies to them, trying to put them to sleep. Most Christians seem to be half-asleep spiritually. They are sleepwalking through life. I know if I stay here long enough, I will become like that. And I don't want that."

It was obvious that even though she was safe and comfortable in the United States, she was not happy with her spiritual life. A couple of months later, she came to my office to talk to me. She did not come to get counsel from me. She had already made up her mind.

"I have decided to go back to Iran and serve the underground church," she declared. "I know it is dangerous, and I may get arrested. I know life will be hard, but I prefer to be there and have a sweet and intimate relationship with Jesus than being comfortable and secure here: struggling to stay alert and not fall asleep spiritually."

She returned to Iran, where she puts her life on the line daily. She walks closely with Jesus in the midst of danger as she serves the underground church.

We Christians in the West must wake up. Jesus wants His church alert and strong. He wants it to influence

We Christians in the West must wake up. Jesus wants His church alert and strong.

the society around it naturally, through day-to-day relationships. When Jesus is on the throne in Iran, the whole nation will be a large church.

When He sets His throne in Iran, the church and society will be so intermingled that they will become one. The church's influence in the community will be strong, yet natural. It will not be limited to a church building. Church leaders will be community leaders—naturally.

The church will serve society. It will do more than hold great services. To get there, we must be careful how we are building the church in Iran. Are we building a church by using the blueprint of our past experiences? Should we give them a model of Christianity and church that has not worked well in the West? Or should we give them a blueprint of what the Lord intends for the future?

We should see with our spiritual eyes that Iran will be an example of what a nation ruled by Jesus can look like. Leaders from around the world will learn from its example. Many will travel to Iran to see what does a nation looks like when Jesus is its King.

Of course, Jesus cares for everyone. He won't rule in Iran and forget the rest of the world. Under His kingship, Iran will bless and influence other nations. Iran will be a great mission force in the world.

3. *Marketplace Transformation:* When lives and families are transformed, the marketplace will be affected too. Most Christians do well on Sunday, but they struggle to live out their faith in the workplace on Monday.

I planted an Iranian church in Northern California and then pastored it for 23 years. My congregation looked so good on Sundays. Every member looked like an exemplary Christian—especially in front of me. But then I heard how some people were behaving in the workplace, and I was heartbroken. It is so easy for Christians to partition their lives into the spiritual and the secular.

When Jesus rules, he destroys religiosity. In the Sermon on the Mount (Matthew 5-7), we see how He stands against religiosity. He confronts religious leaders and *everyone* whose public and private faith practices do not match.

The backbone of a healthy economy is honesty and trust.

The backbone of a healthy economy is honesty and trust. After over forty years of Islamic rule, the economic infrastructure of Iran is almost destroyed because of deception, dishonesty, kickbacks, corruption, and fraud. But when Jesus transforms Iran and sets His throne there, we will see trust and honesty restored, at the highest possible level.

Truth and love are the foundations of His Kingdom. The majority of the population will be Christians who want to glorify the Lord and serve others with everything they have. Greed and selfish ambitions will vanish.

Under this system, the economy will flourish. Under Jesus's rule, Iran will become a wealthy nation that will lend money to other nations and not borrow (Deuteronomy 15:6). When God promises "But it will come about in the last days that I will restore the fortunes of Elam" (Jeremiah 49:39), I see that as a natural result of His ruling Iran according to the previous verse (Jeremiah 49:38).

Since this transformation has already started in Iran, we must be careful to build His Church on the right foundation. We must teach these millions of new converts that Jesus rules all areas of their lives, so their faith must be naturally manifested in their workplaces. They must learn that everything they have belongs to the Lord. It was given to them so they can glorify Him and serve others.

Through our satellite broadcast, we are teaching these values to families. We are teaching businesspeople that their calling to the marketplace is as valid as a pastoral calling. We are inspiring them to make Jesus the true owner of their businesses, and to use their money and influence to advance His Kingdom.

Some are already responding. The Holy Spirit is stirring many of them to accept their calling and take action. The marketplace transformation has already begun. We have identified and are discipling leaders in business who have accepted that call.

Last year, in one of our live satellite TV broadcasts, I talked about being called as a businessman. I said, "Some of you are gifted by God to make money. Whatever you are touching is prospering and turning into gold. But you want to do something great for the Lord. You are successful, but you are not happy. Something is missing. All that money does not mean much to you. I want to tell you that what is missing in your life is responding to His call to serve. God has gifted you and called you to make money for Him and build His kingdom through your presence and witness in the marketplace, and through your money."

A few minutes after the broadcast, a businessman from Iran called. He said, "You were talking about me. God has gifted me to make money. People easily trust me and give me money for business. Tonight, the Holy Spirit talked to me.

"My goal is to be able to make enough money so that I can live on 10 percent and give 90 percent away. Someday, I want to give one million dollars annually to the Lord's work."

We have been guiding and discipling this businessman to help him fulfill his calling.

4. *Media Transformation:* Media is a powerful tool. It has been shown that what impacts a society the most is media.

For good or bad, media has the power to define a society's values and create its norms. It has the power to destroy a culture or build it. He or she who controls the media controls society and its future.

Dictators and tyrants around the world know this. That is why authoritarian countries have media that is controlled by the state. In Iran, media is directly controlled by the office of the Supreme Leader. According to Iran's constitution, the head of the Radio and TV ministry is appointed by the Supreme Leader.

To be clear, by media, we do not mean TV only. Media covers a wide range of technologies and communication vehicles, including books, newspapers, the internet, radio, mobile technology, and more.

In the United States, media has the utmost power over society. It has the power to change the opinions and the value systems of the society without the society knowing that their opinion and values systems are being changed! It has the power to define what is right and what is wrong.

Many believe that US elections are impacted, guided, and even engineered by the media. Presidents are elected in the United States, not just because of their opinions and policies, but also because of how well they use the media.

In today's world, you can't lead any country while ignoring the media. The media is an important tool for any leader. Therefore, when Jesus sets His Throne in Iran, the media will reflect that.

This does not mean Iran will be a society where Christians force their values on others through media, implementing Christian censorship by passing laws on how media operates. Such a top-down religious dictatorship wouldn't be much different from today's Iran. This is not Jesus's way. His plan for impact is bottom-up. He starts by changing individuals and families. That will impact and transform the society in a deep and wide way. Then that societal change will naturally be expressed through media.

So far, much of the media has been used by our enemy, Satan, to destroy what is good and godly in the world. But when Christ rules, the media will be sanctified and used to build values and heal the nations.

If the media can be used to destroy, it can be used to build. Instead of being used to share bad news as it is today, it will be used to share the Good News.

You may ask, "Yes, but who will watch this new media?" Good question. Of course, when we ask that, our point of reference is today's media, which operates in a society that is not ruled by Jesus. But in the future, media will be consumed by a majority who are truly redeemed. They have the heart and mind of Christ. But it is more than that. They will not only watch it; they will demand it.

"But won't that media be boring?"

Good question! We share that concern, because our point of reference is the current religious media, which tends to lack creativity, appeal, and the power to attract. It may be hard for us to believe that a movie can be popular without foul language, nudity, sex, and violence.

Media's power is in its storytelling.

Our current definition of Christian media has limited our creativity and imagination. This has reduced the appeal and effectiveness of our programming.

Media's power is in its storytelling. Most of the Old Testament, the Gospels, and the book of Acts are full of stories. His stories in the Gospels are short, interesting, exciting, engaging, believable, and dramatic—with vivid imagery. And the stories are often open-ended, with no clear conclusion. They pose important questions, rather than providing pat answers.

When Jesus sets His throne in Iran, the media will become an extension of His earthly storytelling ministry. I believe Christians who are free from self, the negative power of the culture, and dry religiosity, can, must, and will produce media pieces that are creative, interesting, and impactful beyond measure.

Meanwhile, on the way to becoming a Christian nation, we need to use media in a new and creative way to impact Iran with the Gospel. We need more than good TV preachers. We need to broadcast powerful, life-changing prayer and worship services.

And that's not all. We need creative storytelling and humor. Jesus used both. My heart aches when I see today's Christian media for the most part, failing to impact lives.

My daily prayer is that the Lord will graciously provide the right people and the finances to make our satellite channel all it can be. I specifically pray for geniuses who are highly gifted and called by God to join us and enable us to use media to impact Iran for the Lord.

Sometimes the Lord has answered. Highly talented people have crossed our path, but we could not afford them. The cry of my heart has been, "Lord, please provide finances so we can do this."

If the world, in order to sell a product or service, can produce a 30-second commercial that brings us to tears, why can't we Christians, by the power and creativity of the Holy Spirit, produce short films that will touch people so deeply that they will make life-changing decisions? I believe we can.

5. *Arts and Sports Transformation:* Celebrities in any society have the power to influence people. Heroes can come from any segment of society, but those from sports or the arts tend to be major role models.

When these people speak out on a subject, no matter how little they know about it, it gets printed, quoted and acted upon by multitudes. Nobody impacts the youth and the next generations more than today's celebrities from the arts and the world of sports.

Nobody impacts the youth and the next generations more than today's celebrities from the arts and the world of sports.

Most of these celebrities may not be heroes to us Christians, but they wield tremendous influence on their followers. They are admired and emulated.

Artists impact society by the work they do and by their celebrity status. Have you ever seen a movie or heard a song that has impacted your life? Do you remember a movie or a song that stayed with you for months and changed how you look at life and the issues you are facing? Of course you do.

Even though months and years have passed, you still remember how that song or movie made you feel. You may not be able to articulate how it impacted your life, but it did. That is the amazing transformative power of media. It impacts the lives of masses.

Unfortunately, many celebrities and artists are not good societal role models. They are more destructive than constructive. Because of that, we Christians may have developed a dislike of any kind of celebrity or well-known person—Christian or non-Christian.

But the media will always raise up and promote celebrities. Some secular media promote anti-Christian celebrities.

Traditionally, we have expected sports celebrities to have high moral standards and exemplary character. They should be role models, especially to the younger generation.

However, in recent years, most "champions" have not been good role models. They have been a negative impact on the younger generation.

As Iran has started its transformation process, we see people becoming more hungry and ready for good role models. I pray for (and expect) a new generation of arts and sports figures to rise in Iran, people who know the Lord and reflect their faith in all they do.

I know a young Christian artist who is popular among Iran's youth. Most of her songs don't mention Jesus directly, but they reflect a Christian message. She shares her faith whenever she can in her concerts. She boldly proclaimed her Christian faith when she was interviewed by the Persian Voice of America.

But she is also heavily criticized by many Iranian pastors. They seem to demand, "If you are a Christian, then sing only Christian songs. Don't sing any songs that aren't specifically about Christian faith. Do not mingle with the secular crowd; they are sinful and corrupt. Unless you repent and do what we say, we won't give you a platform in our churches, or on our Christian TV programs."

Yes, we should be careful about whom we allow to minister in our churches and via our media. Not everyone who talks about love has love. Not everyone who talks about God knows Him. One can sing about morality and lead an immoral life.

But how do we transform arts and sports if we reject our most talented young artists, who can influence that domain for Christ? Why don't we mentor our young, emerging artists rather than reject them and leave them alone to fight their wars by themselves in the secular media?

The Lord is raising up a new generation of talented and committed young men and women of God in Iran. This is a wonderful work of God. It is happening despite the persecution by the government, and opposition by many Iranian pastors.

I have cried listening to the beautiful and touching worship songs by a 15-year-old abused young man, composed secretly in his room in a small Iranian city. (He worked in secret because his parents opposed his faith.) We must recognize art like this as works of God. We must help emerging young anointed artists like this fulfill their God-given missions.

What will arts and sports look like when Jesus is on the throne in Iran? Will arts and sports exist? Will we have celebrities? I believe we will, but the criteria for being a celebrity will be different. When the values of a society change, a new breed of celebrity will emerge.

Remember, a celebrity is someone society admires. If the Gospel has transformed a society and the Bible has shaped its value system, that will affect celebrity culture. People who demonstrate faith, character, and values will be admired. They will be the heroes.

Iran's future celebrities will love the Lord and His people passionately. They will be uniquely gifted, and they will know that God has given them gifts to serve Him and His Kingdom. They will be humble, yet confident and serious about their mission to influence the world.

6. *Education Transformation:* Schools are a primary source of education for the next generation. Students learn more than math and science; they learn values and moral standards too. The US educational system has been deteriorating as our family structure and social system have failed. America's social fiber is disintegrating, and we are losing our reputation for the best secondary schools and universities in the world.

This educational revival will produce the best school system. Students will seek more than a degree. They will glorify the Lord by reaching their maximum potential.

When a society is transformed by the Lord and He rules there, as Iran will be soon, the education system will be reformed—and not from top-down, by the government's initiative, but from bottom-up, by people's initiative.

One distinctive trait of such a society is a zeal for excellence. When the Lord saves us, He sets us free from self, laziness, and mediocrity. A Christian free from inner conflicts and wounds that drain energy and creativity is enabled to do all things and do them with excellence.

This educational revival will produce the best school system. Students will seek more than a degree. They will glorify the Lord by reaching their maximum potential.

Someday soon, when Jesus is the King of Iran, His rule will be reflected in excellent schools. Masses of people, saved and transformed, will joyfully set up an education system that reflects His character, equipping the younger generation to do His will.

7. *Government Transformation:* Most people think that to change a nation, we must change its government. This is not Jesus's way.

When Jesus came to earth, the people lived under the Rome's oppressive government, as well as the abusive power of the religious leaders. The people thought they needed a political revolution, a new government. That's why they tried to make Jesus a king by force (John 6:15).

However, Jesus never sought to topple the political or religious power structures. He told the people, "You must be born again" (John 3:7). He focused on radically transforming the lives of a few. Then he used the transformed disciples to change the world.

Jesus did not initiate a political revolution. Those in power tried to stop this movement, fearing it would undermine their power. They used violent persecution, but they couldn't stop Jesus. The world was changed by Jesus' method: transforming the nations by transforming lives.

Today's Iranians understand that changing the government won't heal the nation. They tried revolution more than forty years ago, and things did not get better. They got worse.

In my broadcasts I often say, "Changing the government without changing the heart of people is useless. A change of government cannot heal your relationship with your wife. A new government cannot restore your relationship with your children. With

The world was changed by Jesus' method: transforming the nations by transforming lives.

a new government, you will still be struggling with your anger, depression, and addiction. You do not need a new government; you need a new heart."

Most Iranians agree with me!

To transform a country, we must make sure that we reach the masses. Of course, those in power also need to hear the Gospel and be saved. But that cannot be our main strategy.

Jesus changes governments by changing people. When Jesus establishes His throne in Iran, He will not appoint Christian leaders to government positions and ask them to transform Iran into a Christian country. Instead, He will rule in the hearts of people whose lives are transformed in such a way that emerging government leaders will reflect that change of heart, and a change of values. Only godly officials, who are the best servant leaders in the country, will rise up to rule the nation under Jesus.

HOW ARE YOU BEING TRANSFORMED?

To be transformed, we must be discipled correctly. Transforming a nation begins with us. Change doesn't happen by default. We must learn to be salt and light in each of the seven arenas we have just discussed.

I often hear, "Politics is dirty and ungodly" or "There is so much filth in media." They are no place for a good Christian to be. They do not realize that they are agreeing with ungodly and anti-Christian demonic voices that proclaim, "You must leave it to us to rule the country. You should gather in your church buildings and have a good time. And when you gather, make sure that you limit your discussions to spiritual matters that do not relate to your society and its government."

Friends, this thinking is wrong. God calls each of His children, including you and me, to be influencers throughout society. He may have already positioned you in one of the seven areas. Or, perhaps He is calling you to step out by faith and fulfill your mission in life in one of those seven areas. Catherine May Ironside did, and her tombstone can still be seen in the courtyard of the Vank Armenia Church in Isfahan, Iran. It reads:

Catherine May Ironside

Medical Missionary in Persia from 1905

Beloved daughter of the late

Edmond and Mary Ironside

Passed Away Nov 11, 1921, Age 49

She heard the call *"Come Follow"* that was all

Earth's joy drew dim, her soul went after Him

She rose and followed – that was all

Will you not follow if you hear the call?

CHAPTER 14

HOW DO WE GET THERE FROM HERE?

IRAN IS UNIQUE. For more than forty years, the nation has been led by clerics who implemented Islamic law. Many other Islamic nations that are ruled by secular governments hold a utopian fantasy: If our country becomes Islamic, things will get better. Iran's people know better. They can say confidently, "We tried Islamic rule in our country. It does not work."

The Christian faith is based on the Bible, which emphasizes love and kindness. The value of individuals is established by God, and freedom of choice is so fundamental that it was given to humankind by God from the beginning—in the Garden of Eden.

Dictatorship is bad, but religious dictatorship is worse. Remember the Middle Ages and how Christian dictators ruled with brutality, corruption, usurpation of power, and violence.

It happened even though the Christian faith is based on the Bible, which emphasizes love and kindness. The value of individuals is established by God, and freedom of choice is so fundamental that it was given to humankind by God from the beginning—in the Garden of Eden.

If Christian dictatorship led to many atrocities, then Islamic dictatorship shall lead to even worse behavior—because the Quran commands violence against those who do not surrender to the will of Allah.

When Christian dictatorship became unbearable, the Reformation started, and many came to true faith in Christ. Now that Islamic dictatorship has become intolerable, many Iranians are coming to Christ. That is why Christianity is growing faster in countries led by dictators. People who live under a dictatorship value the freedom that living under King Jesus offers them.

There is a beautiful Persian worship song that says:

The kings of this earth
Take lives to become sultan of the world
But my King
Gave his life to become the Sultan of my heart.

In Iran, the Supreme Leader has the ultimate say in all matters of life. He controls the government and the personal lives of the people. What he says becomes the law of the land. He can remove or appoint any person at any level of government at any time—even those elected by the people. He can establish any law and cancel the laws passed by the parliament—even though parliament members are chosen by the people.

Yes, there are elections in Iran. But the candidates must be approved by the Guardian Council, which approves only people who profess total obedience to the Supreme Leader. And even after they are elected, they (including the president) have no true power.

Iran's people know this. They accept it as part of their reality.

They know that any effort to make political changes will be crushed mercilessly.

The Supreme Leader is the "Vali Faghih," meaning he represents God on earth. Any person opposing him is classified as an "enemy of God," a crime punishable by death.

THE ONLY HOPE LEFT IS JESUS

People are afraid and hopeless. Those in power make sure that they stay that way. The government publicly hangs people for minor offenses, in an effort to instill terror in everyone's heart.

For example, in June 2014, 49-year-old Gholamreza Khosravi was hanged in public for the "crime" of sending money to support an opposition group. His official charge was "enmity against God."[13]

Despite their fear (and their poverty), many of our viewers want to support our ministry. But they have no way to do it. They cannot use banks, and if they are caught sending money through a third party, they will be charged with being "an agent of the foreign government." They will be jailed or executed.

Iran's people have no hope that this violent oppression will be lifted any time soon. There is no political leader who inspires any hope for the future. The Islamic government makes sure that any emerging political leader (with the potential to become popular and pose a threat to the status quo) is quickly killed or arrested.

Imagine living in a country that squashes your every hope. Today, Iran's people can't even afford necessities like food, gas, or rent.

Will the people rise and take over the government by force? This is unlikely; Iran's people hate violence.

Please understand I am talking about the people, *not* the government. The Islamic government will use violence to the extreme, for any reason, and at any time. Iran's people know that this brutality is rooted in Islamic beliefs. The government represents Islam, so rejecting the government naturally leads to rejecting Islam.

I will say it again: Iranians abhor violence—a very anti-Islamic attitude. Thus, there is little chance of the people uniting behind a violent and bloody revolution. The government will change only if it implodes or there is a coup by the Revolutionary Guards. Thus, the violent government oppression continues.

Nevertheless, Iran's churches are growing rapidly, despite the violent persecution, because the hope of the Gospel is more powerful than government's oppression. Jesus is showing up. He's inviting Iranians to trust Him despite their current circumstances. He is showing them that their true enemy is not the government, but Satan, who is using Islam to oppress and enslave them. Ephesians 6:10-13 encourages us, "Finally, be strong in the Lord and in the strength of His might. Put on the full armor of God, so that you will be able to stand firm against the schemes of the devil.

"For our struggle is not against flesh and blood, but against the rulers, against the powers, against the world forces of this darkness, against the spiritual forces of wickedness in the heavenly places. Therefore, take up the full armor of God, so that you will be able to resist in the evil day, and having done everything, to stand firm."

EVERY EMERGING HOPE IS VIOLENTLY CRUSHED

In Iran's 2009 presidential election, there was a ray of hope that things could change a little. One candidate, Mir-Hossein Mousavi, was considered "moderate." He was not a revolutionary and did not advocate any major changes.

But Iranians were so oppressed and desperately hopeless that they were ready to hang on to a little glimmer of hope. So they rallied around him. Mousavi was one of "them." He had been prime minister of Iran for two terms in 1980s.

He was tested and known by top clergy. They had approved his candidacy, which means he had proven to be submissive to the Supreme Leader. However, he promised a little freedom—like less-strict dress code— and that made him a favorable alternative.

When all the candidates are extreme hardliners, anyone who is a bit moderate will stand out. Iranians wanted Mousavi in power, even though they knew he would bring no major change. But they hoped for even a little less harshness.

So, the people (especially the younger generation) rallied around Mousavi. The clergy in power panicked. He "lost" a fixed election to Ahmadinejad and was placed under house arrest. The government also came down hard on his supporters. Many were arrested and killed. Some were raped and killed in prison, and the government leaked the atrocities, in an effort to terrorize the population. Four young Kurdish men were publicly hanged for being "enemies of God." The official explanation? "We told them not to come on streets to protest, and they did. So they are executed."[14]

After the 2009 election, the Iranian population lost almost all hope for change. Some gave their lives for apparently nothing. Others decided that change was not worth the effort.

A new wave of protests started in December 2017, and those protests continue today. It started because of economic hardship, and it has spread to more than 200 cities. By the beginning of 2020, more than 1,500 young people had been killed on streets. Another 12,000 were arrested.

In 2009, people protested, "Where is my vote?" In 2017, they were saying, "Where is my bread?" But since 2019, they have been protesting against the Islamic government and Islam itself.

Iran's government has ruled by control and deception for more than forty years. When leaders fear that the people have become hopeless to the point of revolt, they offer a candidate who promises change and pretends to care for people. But after the election, nothing changes. The same policies remain in place for another eight years. This deception started with President Khatami more than 25 years ago, and it's been perpetuated by President Hassan Rouhani.

By design, the Islamic government made General Qasem Soleimani a national hero who saved Iran from all its foreign enemies, including ISIS. Unlike other government officials, this leader from the Islamic Revolutionary Guard Corps was liked and respected by the people. The government planned to make him the president of Iran via the 2021 election. This gave the people more false hope.

Soleimani's assassination in January 2020 saved the world from planned terrorist activities, and it saved the Iranian people from another eight years of false hope, deception, and Islamic rule.

NO SEPARATION OF CHURCH AND STATE

Iran is stepping away from Islam—permanently. This rejection didn't happen overnight. It took the people more than forty years to conclude, "Islam is not our solution; it is our problem."

This wasn't an emotional conclusion; it was based on decades of observing and questioning the Islamic government and Islam itself.

There is a growing movement among Iran's youth, who are saying, "If we want to have a future, we must *get rid of* Islam." Yes, there is a growing militancy against Islam among Iranians who are Muslims by birth only.

Protests have become common in many Iranian cities. They aren't going away; they are increasing in frequency and size. Once, people protested only about economic problems. Today, they protest against the government, the Supreme Leader, and Islam itself. They persist, even in the face of imprisonment, torture, and death.

That is how desperate they are. Many youth protest in the streets, knowing they may never return home. When I talk to them, I hear "I don't care about this life anyway. I live a miserable life with no hope and no future. I am not afraid to die."

The suicide rate among Iranian youth is quite high. Suicides used to take place in the privacy of homes, but now some young people hit the streets to protest with suicidal tendencies.

History is in God's hands, but everything that happens is not in His will. He wants none to perish (2 Peter 3:9), but He can use all things to accomplish His goal, which is bringing His lost sons and daughters back to His presence.

In 1979, Iran's people wanted Islam. God allowed them to have an Islamic government, knowing that this would reveal the true face of Islam. He knew that Islam would bring people to a point where they would want His Son, Jesus. He knew this had to happen so that His prophecy in Jeremiah 49:38 would be fulfilled.

When I look at Iran, I see God's power and love. He is saying to humankind, "Go ahead. Use your freedom to make this world a miserable place to live. I love you so much, and I am so powerful that I will use even your wrong choices to bring you to salvation."

IRANIANS LOVE AMERICANS

The media can make you believe, "Oh, we're at war with Iran, and they hate us." That's not true.

What do the people of Iran really want? If there was a referendum today, an overwhelming majority of Iranians would vote for a secular, democratic form of government, American style!

Iran's people love America and everything American.

You may hear "Death to America" chants at government-sponsored rallies, featuring government employees and their families who are forced to participate. These rallies are recorded and sent to Western media. But here is the truth: Iran's people love America and everything American.

In a recent rally, the government put large American flags on sidewalks so that people would step on them. Smartphone videos show that almost everyone took a longer route in order to avoid stepping on the American flag.

There is a disconnect between the government and the people. When the government promotes "Death to America," the people say, "Americans must be good people if our government is against them."

I say with confidence that there is no nation in the world that loves Americans more than Iran. After visiting Iran, my American friend Dr. Ken Fifer told me this:

> "As a mission pastor, I have visited many countries, but I have never been kissed and hugged by so many people as I was in Iran. Once they found out I am American, a crowd would gather around me, welcoming me to their country. I was treated as a celebrity, a pop star. Cars would stop on street, the driver would get out and approach me just to give me a hug and welcome me."

Dr. Fifer continued, "While in Iran, I visited more than ten mosques. They were all empty. I visited one mosque at noon, when the call to prayer filled the whole neighborhood. Hundreds of prayer mats were on the floor, but fewer than five people were there to do their Islamic ritual prayers."

When another of my American friends was about to visit Iran, he asked me for advice. My advice: "Iranians love Americans, and they love Christians. So, wherever you go and whomever you meet, tell them 'I am an American and a Christian.'

"That information will draw a crowd of people, eager to ask you questions."

This friend did not believe me. He said, "No. No. I would not risk that. I know Iranians are against Americans, especially Christians."

A couple of months later, I asked him about his trip to Iran. He said, "You won't believe it. At first, I was afraid. But the day I arrived at my hotel, I gave my American passport to the hotel clerk to register. She looked at my passport and excitedly said, 'Are you from America?' Then she shouted across the lobby, summoning her colleagues.

"She said, 'Hey guys, we have an American guest.' The hotel staff gathered around me. They hugged me and welcomed me.

"The next day, that clerk whispered to me, 'Are you a Christian?'

"I whispered, 'Yes I am.'

"She said, 'Great! Can you get me a Bible?'

"I answered, 'I don't know. I will try.'

"That day, I asked my Iranian friends for a Persian Bible, and they found one. For safety, I wrapped it in a newspaper. The next morning, I went to the front desk and put the wrapped Bible in front of her.

"I got you what asked for," I whispered.

"She was curious. She slowly removed the newspaper. When she saw the Bible, she shouted to the staff: 'Hey guys, he gave me a Bible.'

"The staff gathered around me, saying, 'I want one! Can you get me one?'"

I share this story to reinforce my point: Iranians love Americans. Therefore, American Christians can have a major impact in Iran because Iranian hearts are so open to what Americans have to say.

The God who has opened the hearts of Iranian Muslims to the truth of the Gospel has also changed their hearts toward Americans. That's why Americans have a God-given responsibility to do their part to transform Iran into a Christian nation.

When God changes the heart of a non-believer and you see that he or she likes you, respects you, and is attracted to your attitude and lifestyle, then you are responsible before God to be a witness, to share the Gospel.

Iran is ready for a major transformation. It will be the first Islamic nation that turns to Christ.

By God's grace, He has positioned Iran Alive to have a significant part in that transformation. But we cannot do it alone. We need help from Christian brothers and sisters, churches, and ministries to take advantage of this short window of opportunity to disciple a nation and establish a strong and healthy church there. I am making a Macedonian call: "Come over and help us" (Acts 16:9).

Please visit the Get Involved information (page 244) to learn how you can share in making history in Iran and the Middle East.

VISIONS, DREAMS AND MIRACLES

Jesus loves Muslims and wants them to be saved. He loves the whole world (including Muslims) so much that He died for them. He does not want 1.9 billion Muslims to go to hell. That is one-fourth of the world population! I am sure He is disturbed that His Church is afraid of Muslims, to the point of ignoring them. He sees that only 1 percent of missionary budgets goes to serving 1.9 billion Muslims. So, out of love, He springs into action and does something special: He appears to them in visions and dreams. He miraculously answers Muslims' simple prayers. He heals them.

Seeing Jesus in visions, dreams, and miracles, happens so often that it has become normal to them. Sometimes I feel that if you want to see Jesus these days, you have to be a Muslim! He is favoring them so much that it looks like He is running a special for them.

Jesus is telling all of us, "Hey, wake up and look. See how much I love Muslims. I have done my part to save them: I died on the cross for them. I am appearing to them in visions and dreams, and I am healing them all the time. What else do you expect me to do? Now it is your turn: Go and share the Gospel."

God is moving in Iran, and many people are coming to Christ. Something big, eternal, and historic is happening!

IS YOUR HEART ALIGNED WITH GOD'S?

If we align our hearts with God, we will love what He loves. We will do what He does. Do you love Muslims? Maybe you are afraid of them or even dislike them? Maybe you do not hate them, but are you indifferent to the fact that all face eternal destruction in hell?

The spirit of Islam is fear and hatred. So, if you are afraid of Muslims or hate them, perhaps you have surrendered to that dark spirit.

If so, pray that the Lord will set you free from the spirit of fear and hatred and give you His heart and His Spirit instead.

Another question: Has anybody in your life—at work, at school, among the family, neighbors or friends—seemed especially fond of you? If so, did you sense that respect and admiration? Isn't it great when someone wants to be around you, to be your friend?

This is a God thing. God put those feelings about you into someone's heart. And that means you are responsible before God to connect with those people and influence their lives for Him. He wants you to show them godly love and share the good news with them. He has prepared a harvest for you; do your part to gather it.

CHAPTER 15

THE PAST AND FUTURE OF IRAN IN THE BIBLE

IF I WERE to ask you who the President of the United States of America will be in 150 years, you would shake your heads. None of us knows who he or she will be.

I always ask this question when I speak at conferences, because most people do not know that in the Bible, God gave Persia (Iran) the name of their future king 150 years before he came into power.

Iran's "Great Awakening" may be happening now, but its seeds were planted during reign of King Cyrus, as recorded by the prophet Isaiah in chapter 45.

Iran's "Great Awakening" may be happening now, but its seeds were planted during reign of King Cyrus, as recorded by the prophet Isaiah in chapter 45.

Iran has a rich spiritual history (recorded in the Bible) that dates back to Genesis 10:22, where Elam is listed as the first son of Shem.

THE SPIRITUAL HISTORY OF IRAN

We explored biblical prophecy about Iran (from Ezekiel 38 and Jeremiah 49) in Part II, but did you know that five books of the Bible were written in Iran: Daniel, Esther, Nehemiah, Ezra, and Habakkuk.

Did you know that many kings of Persia are mentioned (all positively) in the Bible? This is an amazing contrast, because most of the kings of Israel and Judah are not portrayed positively in God's Word, due to their sin.

Even when the Bible talks about "good kings," like David and Solomon, there is always a "but" that follows. However, there is no negative comment, no "buts" when the Bible talks about Cyrus, Ahasuerus, Artaxerxes, and Darius.

In Acts 2:9 we see that the first three people groups who responded to the Gospel (Parthians, Medes, and Elamites) were all Iranians.

Many books have been written about Iran's spiritual heritage over the years, but I want to highlight a few things before expounding upon the importance of Isaiah 45 and what it means for Iran, the Jews, and the world today.

In Daniel 10:1 we read, "In the third year of Cyrus king of Persia a message was revealed to Daniel, who was named Belteshazzar; and the message was true and *one of* great conflict, but he understood the message and had an understanding of the vision."

Daniel is in Iran. King Cyrus is on the throne. Daniel has been mourning. He is fasting and has no strength left. As he falls into a deep sleep, an angel touches him and wakes him up to comfort him. He says:

> "Do not be afraid, Daniel, for from the first day that you set your heart on understanding *this* and on humbling yourself before God, your words were heard, and I have come in response to your words.

But the prince of the kingdom of Persia was withstanding me for twenty-one days; then behold, Michael, one of the chief princes, came to help me, for I had been left there with the kings of Persia. Now I have come to give you an understanding of what will happen to your people in the latter days, for the vision pertains to the days yet *future*" (Daniel 10:12-14).

The prince of Persia is one of two evil princes mentioned in the Bible—the other is the prince of Greece—and they are both mentioned in Daniel 10.

Here we read that the prince of Persia has great power and is able to thwart God's messenger angel who was dispatched to help Daniel. In fact, Michael, the chief prince, has to come and help him fight against the prince of Persia, so that the angel can get to Daniel, who has been fasting for twenty-one days. To better understand this passage, let's go back even further.

KING CYRUS: ONE REASON FOR WHAT GOD IS DOING IN IRAN TODAY

King Cyrus is a type of Christ. Isaiah prophecied his birth by name and described major events of his life 150 years before he was born. Consider Isaiah 44:28:

"It is I who says of Cyrus, "He is My shepherd!
And he will perform all My desire.:
And he declares of Jerusalem, 'She will be built,'
And of the temple, 'Your foundation will be laid.'"

In Isaiah 45:1-7 we read:

"Thus says the LORD to Cyrus His anointed, Whom I have taken by the right hand, To subdue nations before him and to loose the lions of kings; To open doors before him so that gates will not be shut: I will go before you and make the rough places smooth; I will shatter the doors of

> bronze and cut through their iron bars. I will give you the treasures of darkness and hidden wealth of secret places, So that you may know that it is I, The LORD, the God of Israel, who calls you by your name. For the sake of Jacob My servant, And Israel My chosen one, I have also called you by your name; I have given you a title of honor though you have not known Me. I am the LORD, and there is no other; Besides Me there is no God. I will gird you, though you have not known Me; That men may know you from the rising to the setting of the sun that there is no one besides Me. I am the LORD, and there is no other, The One forming light and creating darkness, causing well-being and creating calamity; I am the LORD who does all these."

God calls Cyrus "my shepherd." God planned for Cyrus to come to power, with strong financial resources and a heart for the Jews. Cyrus allowed the people to return to Israel and even gave them financial support to build their temple. This occurred right on time, at the end of the seventy-year captivity prophesied in Jeremiah 29:10.

The Bible tells us that a remnant returned to Israel, but many stayed in Iran for centuries. God used Babylon to punish Israel by taking them into captivity, but He used Iran to bless them, to set them free to return home and rebuild the temple. Iran is blessed (and will continue to be blessed) because they blessed Israel.

Iranians don't hate the Jews. They hate their enemy, the prince of the kingdom of Persia: Islam. Why else would God give us a glimpse of an enemy so powerful that it could thwart Michael the archangel? Michael and Gabriel are the only angels mentioned by name in the Bible. (Gabriel is a messenger for God, while Michael is a mighty warrior.)

For centuries, Iran has been a stronghold for Islam, but it wasn't always that way. And things will change in the future. The enemy does not want Iran to be saved and to fulfill its prophetic and historical destiny of bringing salvation to the Jews. (See Romans 11:11.)

God says He will not forget the smallest thing we do for Him. Even when we give a glass of water in His name, He will reward it. So, imagine how richly he will reward someone who sets His people free and blesses them with financial resources and commissions them to rebuild their temple in Jerusalem.

In Genesis 12:3, God says to Abraham, "I will bless those who bless you, and the one who curses you I will curse." God doesn't take that promise lightly, and it has no expiration date.

Throughout the Bible, we find many nations who qualify for "the one who curses you, I will curse." Over the centuries, Jews have suffered at the hands of other nations. The Holocaust was not a one-time event; the Jews have endured many massacres and genocides.

However, the only nation that clearly exemplifies "I will bless those who bless you" is Iran.

Yes, the Abrahamic blessing clearly applies to Iran. When Cyrus set the Jewish captives free to return to their land, most of them stayed in Iran because they were accepted and were doing well financially. Many, like Daniel, held high governmental positions. The Jews have lived in Iran for centuries. Even after Islam invaded Iran and Jews were persecuted, they ultimately recovered and prospered.

God has never forgotten what Cyrus did, and I believe it is one of the reasons that He promises (in Jeremiah 49:38-39) to save and bless Iran.

Today, most Iranian Jews have left Iran, but in the Shah's time, there were many wealthy Jews who lived in Iran and freely did business.

God has never forgotten what Cyrus did, and I believe it is one of the reasons that He promises (in Jeremiah 49:38-39) to save and bless Iran.

His hand of grace has indeed been extended to bless Iranians spiritually. The physical blessing has to wait, but it will come.

What was promised to Cyrus (see Isaiah 45:1-3) is now finding its spiritual fulfillment. I call it the "Cyrus Anointing." Let's look at these verses again:

> "Thus says the LORD to Cyrus His anointed, Whom I have taken by the right hand, To subdue nations before him and to loose the lions of kings; to open doors before him so that gates will not be shut: I will go before you and make the rough places smooth; I will shatter the doors of bronze and cut through their iron bars. I will give you the treasures of darkness and hidden wealth of secret places, So that you may know that it is I, the LORD, the God of Israel, who calls you by your name."

Today, God's hand is reaching out to help Iran. The spirit of Islam is being subdued. The lion of God, Jesus, is free to roam Iran.

Let's focus on the phrase "to open doors before him so that gates will not be shut." Modern Iran is experiencing an open spiritual door—which nobody can shut—despite the political, financial, and social doors that remain closed.

"I will go before you and make the rough places smooth." God has made the spiritual rough places smooth. Even though it is hard for Muslims to come to Christ, God has made the journey smooth and easy for Iranians.

"I will shatter the doors of bronze and cut through their iron bars." He has broken open the doors of Islam where, for many centuries, Iranian captives have been kept hostage.

"I will give you the treasures of darkness and hidden wealth of secret places, So that you may know that it is I, the LORD, the

God of Israel, who calls you by your name." God is blessing Iran spiritually, beyond anything a human could accomplish. This is one reason we know that God has called Iran by name.

IRAN IS GOING TO BE A SENDING NATION

Iran is going to be a missionary-minded "sending nation." This is a natural outcome of God setting His throne there.

I can't imagine He would say, "Okay, this area is transformed, and now I'm satisfied. I don't care about the rest of the world."

No! That's not God's heart. He is a sending God.

Jesus was sent to earth, and He sends us. He says, "As the Father sent me, I also send you" (John 20:21).

God always wants His Kingdom to expand. He always cares for the whole world. He wants everyone saved. When He says He will set His throne in Iran, it's only natural to expect that Iran will become a sending nation that will spread God's Word and His blessing to the whole world.

Jesus came for the Jews and the gentiles. He promises to set His throne in Jerusalem (Jeremiah 3:17) and Elam (Jeremiah 49:38). If He came for the Jews and the gentiles, could His throne for the Jews be in Jerusalem, while His throne in Iran will mainly be for the gentiles?

Paul writes about this in Romans 11: "I say then, they [the Jews] did not stumble so as to fall, did they? May it never be! But by their transgression salvation *has come* to the Gentiles, to make them jealous" (verse 11).

Iran is already at the forefront of fulfilling that prophecy.

Iran is already at the forefront of fulfilling that prophecy. This is not a carnal jealousy, but a biblical and spiritual jealousy. The Jews will be jealous because of what God is doing in Iran. Iran's church is growing due to a movement of God's Spirit.

Thank God that the Jews have started to come to Jesus at an unprecedented rate, but the Church is not growing in Israel like it is in Iran. Right now, some Muslim-background believers are going to Jerusalem to pray for and evangelize the Jews.

I know some of these believers personally. They have told me about the love, passion, and the burden they have for the salvation of the Jews.

Iranians hearts' (Christian and Muslim) are changing toward the Jews. In Iran, people are praying for the Jews and blessing them. It's a movement that has just begun. Right now, the Jews are, understandably, skeptical. They regard Iran as an enemy who wants to wipe Israel off the map. They are shocked to hear about this change of heart: "You say Iranians love us and are coming to bless us and serve us? Really?"

Imagine you had an enemy who wanted to kill you. Then, suddenly, this person approaches you, saying, "God has changed my heart toward you. I love you and want to do whatever I can to bless you."

How would you feel? Wouldn't you be skeptical, saying, "Maybe this is another scheme to hurt me"?

But the change is real. God is changing the hearts of Iranians. Even while the government encourages people to shout, "Death to Israel" in the streets, many Muslims respond, "Tell us again why should we hate the Jews? What have they done to us? You have harmed us more than they have. You are our enemy, not them."

When Iranians come to Christ, they fall in love with the Jews. It's the power of the Bible, and the power of the Holy Spirit.

Imagine Israel's mortal enemies being transformed into their best friends through the blood of Christ. This must not shock us.

According to the Bible, the past and the future of Iran and Israel are intertwined.

Scripture tells us that the futures of Iran and Israel are tied together because when God said that He will set His throne in Jerusalem and Elam, He brought Israel and Iran to a level place in God's Kingdom. Jews and Gentiles share a similar future with Jesus.

HOW DO YOU RELATE TO YOUR ENEMIES?

May I ask you, how would you feel if your enemy, who once made every effort to destroy you, suddenly changed? What if your enemy showed you love and kindness, asked to become your friend, and started blessing you? How would that impact your life?

But what if the opposite thing happened? Is there someone who—for valid or invalid reasons—considers *you* an enemy? What if he sees that you have suddenly changed your heart and attitude toward him? Now you are being kind. You want God's best for him and want to bless him in practical ways? Imagine how that would impact this person's life—perhaps for eternity.

Perhaps the Lord is bringing somebody to mind right now. Maybe He wants you to take a step of faith and obedience to bless them. We Christians can break the power of a curse with a blessing. We are called to bless those who curse us, and to love our enemies (Matthew 5:44) so that we can overcome evil with good (Romans 12:21).

On another note, have you ever done something for the Lord and His church, without being acknowledged, appreciated, and rewarded? Do you believe that God saw what you did and will reward you for it?

I encourage you to do His will and bless people (even your enemies), even if you receive no gratitude. Even if these people don't return the blessing, the One who counts *will* bless you.

EPILOGUE

WHAT ABOUT PERSECUTION?

IRAN WILL BE a Christian nation—but not without a fight. Iran will face fierce opposition from the enemy: the Prince of Persia.

There is never a big victory without a big war!

As the Church in Iran grows, so does the persecution. Soon, Iran's Islamic government will wake up to the fact that the number of Christians is way beyond what they thought it was—and growing out of control.

That is when there will be a huge new wave of persecution, to halt, even destroy, Christianity in Iran. Satan came to steal and kill and destroy. Nothing less will satisfy him. (See John 10:10.)

Satan is a brutal tyrant who does not give up his territory without a fight. He has used Islam to bring 1.9 billion people—one-fourth of the world's population—under his slavery.

He lies. He uses fear. He uses violence and even death to keep those precious Muslim souls in captivity. Those who dare to walk away from Islam are killed as apostates. This is the reality of

Islam. It is easy to become a Muslim—simply recite a phrase in Arabic—but it may cost your life to leave Islam.

It seems that persecution and suffering are integral parts of God's plan to save the world. Jesus went through persecution and suffering to save the world. The apostles endured persecution and suffering as the Lord used them to spread the message of salvation. As Jesus is calling us to participate in His mission, He is also calling us to participate in His suffering (1 Peter 4:12-13)

Therefore, Iran will not be saved without the Church enduring persecution and suffering. The persecution in Iran has started, and it will get worse.

You may ask, "How is Iran's underground church enduring persecution now, and how will it survive as the persecution intensifies?"

The good news is that the Lord never abandons His persecuted Church. He gives extra grace to persecuted Christians. When He commands His Church to "Go therefore and make disciples of all the nations," He also promises, "I am with you always, even to the end of the age" (Matthew 28:19-20).

THE PERSECUTED CHURCH CAN BLESS US

I love to talk about persecution. There is so much drama in persecution. There is God versus Satan—although God and Satan are not equal. God, the Creative One, created Satan as an angelic being, but Satan chose to rebel against Him.

There is much commotion when good confronts evil. When the light meets the darkness, it creates fireworks.

Today, a fierce physical and spiritual battle is waging. Lives and souls are at stake. When God's power is released to set the captives free, the slave owner, Satan, always fights back. He will never relinquish his slaves without a struggle.

Don't misunderstand me when I say I love to talk about persecution. The suffering that our brothers and sisters go through breaks my heart. But the way they stand up for the Lord (and the way the Lord stands up for them) inspires me and brings joy to my heart. It strengthens my faith and my commitment to the Lord.

I want you to be blessed by the persecuted Church, as I have been. I want you to have compassion for the persecuted Church, to stand up for them and support them in their tribulations.

I want you to be blessed by the persecuted Church, as I have been.

But I also want you to be encouraged and inspired by them and to learn from their boldness for the Lord in the face of adversity.

When the enemy shows up with power and determination to stop and destroy God's Kingdom, the Lord moves with a greater power to protect and overcome.

As Jesus promises, "From the days of John the Baptist until now the kingdom of heaven suffers violence, and violent men take it by force" (Matthew 11:12).

IRAN: A MODERN-DAY BOOK OF ACTS

The book of Acts is happening in Iran right now. I could share many stories of events happening in Iran that are similar to those in Acts.

As in the book of Acts, I am seeing supernatural works of God—visions, dreams, and miracles, all happening in the middle of fierce persecution.

Acts portrays God's grace manifested through His Church by the supernatural works of the Holy Spirit, empowering them to be courageous, faithful, wise, and bold.

We see similar things in Iran: the same persecution and the same grace of God in action.

The good news is that through Jesus' death and resurrection, the battle has already been won!

In my next book, I will share how the book of Acts is being re-enacted in Iran. Iran's top clerics have vowed publicly to "wipe out" and "eradicate" Christianity. But the Lord has vowed, "I will build My church; and the gates of Hades will not overpower it" (Matthew 16:18).

The result is the dramatic story of good and evil meeting face to face. The good news is that through Jesus' death and resurrection, the battle has already been won!

Let's briefly examine five ways the New Testament church in Acts parallels the church in modern Iran:

1. Oppression. In Acts, people were oppressed by those in power. Religious leaders were allies with the Roman government and its powerful military, which oppressed and exploited the people. Religious and government authorities showed no heart, no mercy for the people. Today's Iranian Islamic government wields religious, governmental, and military power to subdue, enslave, and abuse its people. In Jesus's time, oppression made people desperate for change. They looked for a Savior. The same is true in Iran. After forty-plus years of suffering under oppressive Islamic rule, the people are crying out for change, and for somebody who can be their Savior. The oppression in Jesus's time opened people's hearts to His fresh teachings about love, forgiveness, and change from within. It's no wonder that 3,000 people came to Christ on the day of Pentecost. After a lifetime of oppression and abuse, they were ready for something better.

2. Exponential growth of the church. From the day of Pentecost forward, thousands of people came to Christ in Jerusalem. In one generation, the Gospel was spread across the world by Jewish-background believers. We see a similar rate of growth among Iran's churches. At Iran Alive Ministries, we strongly believe that within one generation, Iran's Muslim-background believers will impact their country, the Middle East, and even the whole world.
3. Growing persecution. As the New Testament church grew, it faced increasing persecution. We are seeing the same thing in Iran, and this trend will continue.
4. Visions, dream, signs, and miracles. Supernatural events are common in Acts. We see manifestations of the Holy Spirit everywhere. Similarly, the supernatural has become "natural" in Iran. Interacting with the Holy Spirit has become a normal part of life for most of Iran's Christians.
5. Supernatural faith, courage and boldness. The Christians in Acts did not shrink in fear when persecuted; they stepped out boldly. After Peter and John were arrested and tried, the believers prayed, "And now, Lord, take note of their threats, and grant that Your bond-servants may speak Your word with all confidence, while You extend Your hand to heal, and signs and wonders take place through the name of Your holy servant Jesus" (Acts 4:29-30). The same grace is on the believers in Iran, enabling them to be bold in the face of persecution. It is my prayer to release this book soon.

ALLAH VERSUS JEHOVAH

Here's a story that shows why I am excited about my next book:

I was in Turkey for a week-long intensive underground church leadership training conference. (I am one of the "most wanted" by Iran's Islamic government. They consider me an "enemy of the state," so I can't even visit Iran, let alone train leaders there. I have to bring leaders to a third country—like Turkey—for training.)

These young underground house church leaders were so hungry for teaching that every day for almost 12 hours they sat eagerly under the teaching of a team of instructors, including me. But that was not enough for them.

Every night at about 10, the exhausted teachers would go to their rooms to rest. But not the students. They gathered nightly from 10 pm until 2 in the morning for a passionate prayer and worship meeting, which included singing loudly, dancing exuberantly to the worship music, and composing impromptu worship songs.

On the conference's final night, I watched the people dancing and singing their hearts out.

I thought, *Do they know that tomorrow at the airport, on their way back to Iran, they could be arrested, jailed, and tortured? They are so full of joy and seem to have no concern. Maybe I have not fully taught them about the reality of persecution. Maybe they are being carried by their emotions and do not completely understand the issue of persecution in the Bible, and the price they may have to pay for serving Him under a hostile Islamic government.*

So, I interrupted their prayer and worship session and told them, "Stop! Come and sit down, because I have one last teaching for you."

They stopped and sat down to listen to me. For a half hour, I taught from the Bible about the reality of persecution. I told them that persecution is a normal part of serving God. I was honest with them: "Some of you may be called to give the ultimate price—your life—for your faith."

They listened attentively and respectfully. When I finished, a few of them spoke up: "Pastor Hormoz, please do not worry about us. We know what we have gotten into. When we were Muslims, we were willing to die for Allah, who is distant and cruel. How much more we are ready to die for Jehovah, who is an intimate and loving God. So please don't worry about us."

They continued "By the way, you interrupted our joyful worship and dancing before Jesus. We were having such a great time. Can we go back to doing that?"

Remember, the persecuted Church in Iran needs us, but we also need them. They desire to learn from the Church in the West. They ask eagerly, "Please teach us what you know about the Bible and Christian life."

Remember, the persecuted Church in Iran needs us, but we also need them.

They are eager to learn from us, but we need to learn from *them* about faithfulness, surrender, and loving God. We should emulate their passion for His Kingdom, and their courage in serving Him.

We can bless them, and we can be blessed *by* them. Because we are one body, we need each other.

You will read more about this mutual blessing process in my next book. Until then, you can learn more about how to pray or get involved. Turn to Get Involved on page 244 to connect with me personally.

QUESTIONS FOR REFLECTION

Chapter 1: Death to Shah, Death to America!"

1. Do you practice any spiritual rituals or routines that aren't making a difference in your life? What changes can you make to truly experience God's life-giving power and love?

2. Do you believe your life is unique? Do you have dreams that are yet to be fulfilled? If so, please ask God to help you discover (or rediscover) the purpose behind His design for you. Perhaps you will find that God wants to resurrect your dreams and enable you to fulfill them.

Chapter 2: "You Are an Infidel, and You Will Go to Hell!"

1. Is God asking you to do something difficult, something beyond your comfort zone? What will happen if you say yes to God? What if you say no?

2. Have you read the Bible with a truly open mind, and encountered the Jesus of the Bible? How has the Bible impacted your life so far?

3. Do you believe that all religions are essentially equal, and that they ultimately lead to the same place? Why or why not?

Chapter 3: My Younger Brother Was Executed

1. Does anyone in your family disagree with your spiritual beliefs? Has anyone in your family been persecuted because of their political or spiritual beliefs? What are their reasons? How can you respond to them? How can you convince them with your lifestyle?

2. How do you respond to a crisis in your life? Do you become discouraged, or more committed to God?

3. When you see injustice done to you or someone else, how do you react? Do you blame God, or recommit your life to Him?

4. Which Bible verses have comforted and helped you endure trials? How? What impact did it have on your thoughts, attitudes, and behaviour?

Chapter 4: "I Am Giving You the Honor to Join Me"

1. Donnell and I prayed that God would use us to save Iran, to awaken an entire nation. What impossible dream is God asking you to pray about?

2. Are you currently pursuing your calling, or have you given up on it? Now is the time to recommit your life to the Lord and pursue your calling and God-given vision! It is never too late to say, "Yes," to God!

3. Has it ever cost you anything to follow God? What did you learn from saying "yes" or "no" to Him?

Chapter 5: Getting Kicked Out of the Church I Started

1. Churches should be hospitals for the lost and the hurting, but have you ever been wounded by a church or church leader? Have you ever felt betrayed or abandoned by your church? How did it make you feel? How did you find healing?

2. Do you believe in dreams and visions? Has God ever used dreams or visions to confirm His calling in your life? If not, is this something you would like to receive? Turn to "Get Involved" on page 244 to connect with me personally.

3. Have you ever experienced a breakthrough right after a time of hopelessness and despair? What changed for you?

Chapter 6: Our Switchboard Lit Up Like a Christmas Tree

1. Have you ever been ministered to through media (TV, radio, or the internet)? Do you think God might want you to use the media to reach the world? If so, what venues are open to you, and what will you do about it?

2. Have you ever led someone to Christ? If so, how did it make you feel? If not, what is hindering you from sharing the Good News of Christ?

3. Has God ever asked you to make a big change in your life? If so, what happened?

4. Have you ever felt stuck in your job, ministry, church, or family situation? What did this experience teach you?

Chapter 7: Sixty-Five Family Members Come to Christ

1. What does leaving a legacy of faith look like to you? Are you currently discipling the next generation of believers?

2. Have you ever shared your faith with a friend or family member who believed in a different religion than you? What happened?

3. Do you believe in healing? Have you ever received prayer for healing? Have you ever prayed for someone to be healed in Jesus' name? Why or why not?

4. Have you ever had the honor of leading someone to Christ? If you haven't yet believed in Christ, would you pray the prayer below with me?

> Jesus, I believe You love me and want to save me right now. I believe You love me so much that You willingly went to the cross to pay for my sins. I receive Your love. I receive Your salvation and ask You to forgive me and change me. From now on, I belong to You and You belong to me. My life is Yours. I am Your child and You are My Father. You will never leave me, and I will never leave You. I accept you as Lord, and I surrender my life to You. In Jesus's name. Amen.

If you just prayed this prayer, please turn to Get Involved on page 244 to connect with me personally.

Chapter 8: For the Bible Tells Me So!

1. What is the history of your last name? How did it come to be? What is its meaning?

____

____

____

____

____

____

____

____

____

2. What is the meaning of your first name? When you came to Christ, do you feel the Lord gave you a new name (see Revelation 2:17)? What is it? How does that bless you? What does it say about your value, calling, and future?

Chapter 9: Iran Will Be Attacked

1. Where in your life have you experienced brokenness? How did you respond to it? Did it make you walk away from God or toward God?

2. Looking at your past sufferings, how did God bless you through that? How did He shape you and prepare you for a greater blessing? If you can't answer this, stop, pray, and ask God to reveal to you how He has worked in your life, changed you for better, and blessed you through those sufferings. Write it down and use it to encourage others around you who are suffering and broken.

3. Look at your current sufferings. How is God trying to use them to shape your character, build your faith, deepen your relationship with him, and teach you valuable life lessons? Write this down and look at it often so that you remember what He is doing in you during this season of your life. That will help you not to lose heart.

Chapter 10: There Will Be a Horrible War in Iran

1. Study Hebrews 12:1-11. How does this passage relate to your life today?

2. Have you ever been disciplined by the Lord? How did He discipline you? What was the result? What did you learn about yourself, the world, or Him? How did that change you? What did He remove from your life? What did He add?

3. If you are going through a hard time, ask yourself, Is this God disciplining me? Is the pain of discipline causing you to walk away from God or toward Him? What changes is He trying to bring into your life? You may not feel it, but do you believe He loves you through it?

4. Do you know any Christian who is being discipline by the Lord? Do you know any non-Christian whom God has allowed to go through suffering? How can you reach out to them at this time of need, be a voice of God to them, and help them to look at their lives from His perspective?

Chapter 11: God Will Set His Throne in Iran!

1. Do you know why God created you? What gifts and talents has He given you? What mission do you have in life? If you know it, write it down and pray about it regularly so you will move in that direction. If not, look at your your spiritual gifts, talents, and personality. Then pray to the Lord that He may reveal to you His plans for your life.

2. Have you ever felt a promise in the Bible spoke to you personally? If so, which one? The Bible says that all promises are "yes and amen" in Jesus (2 Corinthians 1:20). Write that promise down and then make life changes, if necessary.

3. Christian life is living in a Kingdom where Jesus is the King. What do you think that means? Is Jesus the King in your life? If not, what changes do you need to make?

Chapter 12: Iran Has the Fastest-Growing Christian Population

1. What do you think a true Christian looks like? What does it look like when Jesus truly becomes the King of one's life?

2. Have you ever experienced revival in your heart and life? How did that happen? How did God prepare you for it, and what ultimately was the result?

3. Are you desperate for Change? What motivates you to make changes in your life? What stops you? Have you surrendered your life to Jesus?

Chapter 13: Back to The Future of Iran

1. To which of the seven areas of transformation has God called you? What has surprised you as you have learned more about Iran? How has that knowledge inspired you?

2. How can you be a change agent in your family, among your friends, and in your workplace? How does God want you to be salt and light?

3. Romans 12 is about how to be transformed and how to be an agent of transformation. Study that chapter and ask the Lord to reveal its life principles.

CHAPTER 14: HOW DO WE GET THERE FROM HERE?

1. In your opinion, how can a nation be changed? Does a nation's transformation start with government, or with the people? What does the Bible say about national change?

2. What do you think "Separation of Church and State" means? How does the BIble say about it? Given this separation, how can the Church impact society?

3. Is there a non-Christian at your workplace, school, or among your friends and acquaintances who seems to like you and respect you? Do you see God's purpose in this relationship? Pray and ask God what He wants you to do to influence that person's life spiritually.

Chapter 15: What Does the Bible Say about The Past and Future of Iran?

1. Is there somebody who believes that you are his enemy, that you are out to get him? Can you identify some of his needs you might be able to meet? Ask God how you can surprise this person by blessing him (or her).

2. Have you ever been treated unfairly by a church or a Christian leader, despite your selfless service and loyalty? Has that stopped you attending church and serving the Lord? God wants to heal your heart and use you in an even greater way. Pray and forgive those who have hurt you. Ask God how He wants to use you in His Kingdom.

3. Do you seek the approval of people? Paul says that by seeking the approval of men, you cannot be a servant of God (Galatians 1:10). Pray and seek freedom from the need for people's approval. Ask the Lord where and how *He* wants you to serve.

NOTES

1. "Elam, Ancient Kingdom, Iran," Encyclopedia Britannica, accessed, November 6, 2019, https://www.britannica.com/place/Elam.

2. "Susa," Study Light, accessed, November 6, 2019, https://www.studylight.org/dictionaries/hbd/s/susa.html.

3. "Iran lawmaker announces a $3 million cash reward for 'whoever kills Trump,'" Fox News, accessed January 22, 2020, https://www.foxnews.com/world/iran-lawmaker-3m-cash-bounty-kills-trump.

4. "Iran, North Korea secretly developing new long-range rocket booster amid talks," Fox News, accessed October 29, 2019, https://www.foxnews.com/politics/iran-north-korea-secretly-developing-new-long-range-rocket-booster-amid-talks.

5. "Did U.S. Cyberattacks On Iran Backfire On American Banks?" Forbes, accessed October 29, 2019, https://www.forbes.com/sites/tomgroenfeldt/2013/06/08/did-u-s-cyberattacks-on-iran-backfire-on-american-banks/.

6. "These 15 countries, as home to largest reserves, control the world's oil," USA Today, accessed November 6, 2019, https://www.usatoday.com/story/money/2019/05/22/largest-oil-reserves-in-world-15-countries-that-control-the-worlds-oil/39497945/.

7. "Natural Gas Reserves by Country," Index Mundi, accessed November 6, 2019, https://www.indexmundi.com/energy/?product=gas&graph=reserves&display=rank.

8. "Huge cost of Iranian Brain Drain," BBC News, accessed October 30, 2019, http://news.bbc.co.uk/2/hi/middle_east/6240287.stm.

9. "Iran's Sharif University's Ranking - Electrical Engineering - Best of the world," YouTube, accessed October 30, 2019, https://www.youtube.com/watch?v=s957W6jomBc.
10. Jason Mandryk, Operation World: The Definitive Prayer Guide to Every Nation (Downers Grove, IL: InterVarsity Press, 2010), 916.
11. "Iran has world's 'fastest growing church,' despite no buildings – and is mostly led by women: documentary," Fox News, accessed October 29, 2019, https://www.foxnews.com/faith-values/worlds-fastest-growing-church-women-documentary-film.
12. "Revival," Merriam-Webster Dictionary, accessed November 12, 2019, https://www.merriam-webster.com/dictionary/revival.
13. "The Great Awakening," U.S. History, accessed November 12, 2019, http://www.ushistory.org/us/7b.asp.
14. "To the Heroic Memory of Gholamreza Khosravi, 4 Years After His Execution by Iran Regime," National Council of Resistance of Iran, accessed November 12, 2019, https://www.ncr-iran.org/en/news/iran-resistance/24845-it-has-been-14-years-since-the-execution-of-gholamreza-khosravi.
15. "Iran executes Kurdish activist," The Guardian, accessed November 19, 2019, https://www.theguardian.com/world/2009/nov/11/iran-executes-kurdish-activist.

ACKNOWLEDGMENTS

MY FIRST WORD of acknowledgment goes to my Lord, Jesus Christ. Thank You for patiently working in me, through me, and for me. You did it all, I am just reporting what You have done.

To my wife, Donnell, who has always supported the hard decisions we made in life together. Thank you for the love and patience you have shown me through the journey of life together. Your prayers and "words from the Lord" have impacted me more than you imagine.

To my children, Hanniel, Jonathan, and Michelle, who have brought so many joyful memories to my life, and to my grand-grand-grand-grandchildren, with this book, I want you all to know where God entered our family line. I pray that you all will know Him, serve Him, and make your life count for Him. I will be cheering for you from heaven.

To Joel C. Rosenberg, your support, encouragement, and friendship have meant so much to me. Your life example of integrity, creativity, and passion has been a great inspiration to me. Thank you for having such a big, God-like heart to include not just the Jews but Gentiles like me in your circle of love.

To my Mom, Shamsi, you taught me to be open-minded and to think objectively. That helped me find the truth in Jesus. By your life example, you taught me to work hard and never give up. After coming to Christ, you were a great example of a disciple. Thank you for all those phone calls you made just to encourage me in serving the Lord. I am honored to call you "Pastor Mom." I saw joy and life in your eyes before you passed away. I look forward to looking at those eyes again in heaven.

To my niece, Haleh, thank you for living as a great example of faith, hope, and love, even to the last day of your life. You died young, but greatly impacted my life (and the life of anybody who knew you) in a deep, lasting, and eternal way, even at your deathbed.

The leaders you trained are now making an impact in Iran and around the world. That is why I dedicate this book to you.

To Jim Dau, Peggy Dau, Cole Richards, Jonathan Eckman, and many other past and present leaders at the Voice of the Martyrs, thank you for standing with me and Iran Alive, even through hard times. I truly have experienced God's grace through you. You have done exceedingly abundantly above all that I have asked or imagined. You did everything needed to help this book get written and published. It could not have happened without you. I am eternally grateful.

To Ron Warren, you were the first to see potential in me and our ministry, Iran Alive. Thank you for your friendship and encouragement. Your God-inspired words of wisdom—written both in my notes and on my heart—have guided me when making key decisions for myself and our ministry. Thank you for seeking to listen to God and do what He asks you to do. I am honored to know you and call you a friend.

To Peter Smith, thank you for your unwavering friendship over the years. You have walked with me and Iran Alive through the valleys and peaks. You have seen my laughter and tears in ministry. Thank you for your example of dedication, consistency, and persistence. Thank you for standing with me and for me.

To Dr. Bryce Jessup, thank you for the education I got at Jessup University by great Bible teachers and leaders, including you. By observing you, I learned a lot about leadership—how to be soft and gentle, yet also firm and determined.

To Renee Fisher, thank you for going beyond editing this book, for always encouraging and patiently guiding me through the process of writing it. Your zeal for the Lord and for this book always warmed my heart.

To the editing team, Dr. Harold Berry and Todd Hafer, thank you for all your hard work to make this book better. Special thanks to Dennis Waterman for great cover design.

ABOUT THE AUTHOR

Because of Iran Alive Ministries' effective satellite television broadcasts to the Middle East and Europe, Joel C. Rosenberg has called Dr. Hormoz Shariat "the Billy Graham of Iran." Iran Alive's ministry reaches millions of people and has brought hundreds of thousands of Muslims to Jesus Christ since its inception.

Dr. Hormoz Shariat was born into a Muslim family in Iran. He came to the United States after the Islamic Revolution of 1979. Dr. Shariat came to Christ while a graduate student in 1980. He holds a PhD in Artificial Intelligence from USC, and a bachelor's degree in Bible and Theology from Jessup University. In 1987, he planted a church in San Jose, California. With hundreds of Muslim converts, it remains one of the largest churches of its kind in the United States.

His passion for Muslims stems, in part, from the murder of his brother Hamraz, who was arrested in Iran at the age of sixteen on a minor political charge. After two years in jail, Hamraz was executed by firing squad. God showed Hormoz that the best way to respond to this tragedy was to dedicate his life to loving Muslims and sharing the Gospel with as many of them as possible.

Christianity Today, *Charisma* and other publications have featured Iran Alive Ministries and Dr. Shariat. He has been a guest on numerous national and international radio and TV programs, including *The 700 Club*. Connect at IranAliveMinistries.org.

GET INVOLVED

If you would like to pray for Iran or learn how to support Iran Alive Ministries, please contact us.

Also, if you prayed the prayer of salvation in this book, please contact me and let me know. I would like to send you a testimony DVD as a gift.

CONTACT INFORMATION

Iran Alive Ministries

PO Box 518

Melissa, TX 75454

(469) 982-0000

info@iranaliveministries.org

Text the word "Iran" to "74784"

to receive more information